Love Letters To My Black Son

Presented By
Jonnita Dockens

Contributing Authors
Alicia Cole, Jonnita Dockens, Dr. Paviella Foster, Osei
Hawkins, Melonee Ferguson, Laquita Maxey, Maria
Muhammad, Yolanda Muhammad, and Freda Sowell

Love Letters To My Black Son.
Copyright © 2021 by Confidante Consulting, LLC

Confidante Consulting, LLC
friend@confidanteconsulting.com
www.lovelettersstomyblackson.com

ISBN: 978-1-7365130-0-2 (Paperback)
ISBN: 978-1-7365130-2-6 (Hardcover)

Library of Congress Control Number: 2021921381

Dedication

This book is dedicated to Black Sons all over the world. You are seen, heard, and loved. A special dedication is extended to the sons of our authors Alif Jr., Basim, Jamal, Jaylen, Jonathan Jesus, John Jr., Jeremiah, Joshua, Osei, Omari, Maveric, Montel, Samad, Sincere, Nathaniel and Matthew.

Table of Contents

Foreword

Sometimes we do not realize how important it is to just hear the words I LOVE YOU! This is especially true when it comes to family and when it comes to our **BLACK SONS**. We assume that they just know we love them because we are their parent. We must make it a habit to open our mouths and say I Love You. We must write it down on paper. We must email it, and say I love you by text message.

In the past love letters were not for our children. However, we must remove that thought because more than ever our **BLACK SONS** need to hear from us that they are worthy. They need to understand that we love them unconditionally. It is very important because the world isn't showing them the love they need.

Our Black sons are surrounded by images and public examples of hatred. We have witnessed this hatred in the murders of so many Black males of all ages. Their lives have been taken in various forms. They have been gunned down by police. During the time, we were writing this book the world was listening to the tragedy of George Floyd's homicide at the hands of a police officer's kneeling on his neck. In addition, to the harm that has been caused on Black sons from police, across the United States we see the lives of Black sons being taking by other Black sons.

The authors of this book welcome you to take a step into their life experience and share their expression of love. After you have read our stories, we encourage you to send an expression of love to a Black son.

CHAPTER 1

THE GREATEST GIFT

BY MELONEE FERGUSON

THE GREATEST GIFT
BY MELONEE FERGUSON

My Dearest Son,

It's with great joy that I write this letter of love to you. May you cherish the spirit of my love.

It was a sunny, beautiful, Tuesday afternoon. I walked into your bedroom to see if you had room in your suitcase to pack the extra comforter, mattress pads, and extra-long twin sheets that were ordered. To my surprise, your clothes were scattered everywhere; shoe boxes were emptied; and your closet was in disarray. You were sitting on your bed playing your video game and you looked at me and said, "I got this Mommy." I didn't know what to think, but I knew we were running out of time. Both you and your dad were driving because we had so much to pack, including your refrigerator and sports stuff. I wanted to make sure you had everything.

I had booked a flight to be there at the same time you two arrived on campus. Additionally, we were on a schedule because you had to be at college at a certain time for orientation. I came back into your bedroom a couple of hours later and you did as you said. Your clothes were meticulously packed; your shirts and jeans were folded; socks were rolled up; shoes were packed as though they were fresh out of the box and the sheets and comforter were packed in another suitcase.

I couldn't believe this day was finally here and I was excited **but** scared. I was excited to know that my only son was going to college, and he will experience college life on his own, learning the good, bad, and indifferent. It felt like just yesterday, I could finally hold the love of my life for the first time. I was scared about your transition to college life, due to the world we live in now, and managing the mindset, values, and beliefs of others. You are my only son, my greatest gift.

The Greatest Gift

When I was carrying you in my womb, I enjoyed every moment of being pregnant. It was like receiving an undiscovered treasure that I couldn't wait to open. The anticipation of unraveling the silk bow which wrapped, hugged, and secured this magnificent box of joy was exciting.

You transformed my body in ways unimaginable. People who saw me from behind wouldn't have thought I was pregnant, but once I turned around it was a different story. I carried you like a precious ball from every Hall of Fame. I was so proud and honored to show such an amazing gift. My eyes were bright, my lashes were bold, and when I blinked, you could feel my smile as it radiated throughout the room. My attire consisted of extra-large blouses and maternity pants with heels that captivated my grace as I carried you. I wasn't your traditional converse or loafer-wearing pregnant mom.

You were born into this world on a bright wintery day in December at 8:54 p.m. I remember that morning. I was up early eating breakfast. I loved to eat pancakes when I was pregnant with you. I was cleaning up the house, and I felt contractions coming on strong. I knew what that meant. It was time to go to the hospital. The roads were slushy with ice, but I remained calm because I didn't want to put any stress on my body. At the beginning of labor, I was anxious for your arrival, but very attentive as the nurse asked me questions. My focus was to remain chilled. Something about labor increased my senses. They were very keen. I could hear every faint sound in the room including the sounds of the minute hand ticking on the clock. You came out of the womb with wide shoulders, straight black hair, thick dark silky eyebrows, and soft round eyes. You were perfect in my eyes. Your father and I named you Maveric. Webster's dictionary defines Maverick as, "an unorthodox or independent-minded person." However, we saw more of you and in you at birth than any dictionary could ever capture. We defined Maveric as ambitious, intelligent, caring, dedicated, and a great leader.

"The peace of my treasure has been discovered and is loved."

It was suggested that I get plenty of rest and that the nurses take you to the nursery with the other infants. I was persistent in keeping you near me as you latched on quickly to breastfeeding. After the delivery, I was moved to my own room on the nursery wing. I remember this day vividly. We enjoyed every moment together as we continued to watch marathons of movies from the hospital bed until we both fell asleep. I recalled a snowy New Year's Eve as I looked out the window in our hospital room that evening. I saw the snow in the array of frozen blooms with the blustery wind raging against the windowpane. And then later, your father called and said he was stuck, and he couldn't come to the hospital. It was a blizzard! It was you and me again and we watched ABC's New Year's Rockin' Eve and celebrated as we rang in the New Year.

Months later, I noticed your breathing pattern was abnormal. One evening I stayed awake all night and watched as you inhaled in shallow rasping breaths through your nostrils. I couldn't bear your struggle. Instinctively, I took you to see your pediatrician the next day. The doctor examined you and I'll never forget the look on her face when she said to me, "Are you ready? There is nothing else I can do for him here; I'm calling the ambulance." The heaviness of an undescribed sorrow came upon my body. My eyes began to well up with tears. I tried to hold them back like a rudderless boat attempting to navigate the cascading waters of Niagara Falls. I bravely looked at the doctor and said, "Let's do this!"

I knew I was unable to drive, so I called your father and told him that I would be leaving the car in the parking lot and riding with you in the ambulance. When the ambulance arrived, two emergency medical technicians came through the pediatrician's office doors with a gurney. I watched them as they gently laid you down and strapped you in with a breathing device across your nose. I didn't want you to see Mommy cry with a look of great sadness in my face. I turned away from you as my eyes began to uncontrollably flood with tears.

I prayed and whispered in your ear that you were not only loved by us but loved by God and He made you strong. The echoing sirens and the waves of the speeding ambulance were new to me. I hadn't experienced these sounds before. We arrived at the hospital where they diagnosed you with a respiratory infection, which I called, "My winter baby blues." We stayed at the hospital for three days, and each day was filled with prayers, breathing treatments, hugs, kisses, and we saw you get stronger and stronger.

Our prayers were answered and the words of Isaiah 41:10 filled us with security saying:

"So do not fear, for I am with you; do not be dismayed, for I am your God. I will strengthen you and help you; I will uphold you with my righteous right hand."

Champion Of My Heart

A champion is a person who focuses on the better good, not only for themselves, but also for others. One who speaks volumes of truth to protect the equal rights of the cause. A person accepted as better than all others in a sport or a game of skill or the winner of first place in a competition. For example, Jackie Robinson broke the color barrier when he became the first Black athlete to play Major League Baseball after joining the Brooklyn Dodgers. Muhammad Ali is recognized as one of the greatest boxers in history; the first fighter to win the world heavyweight championship on three different occasions. And he was known for his social delivery of Black pride and Black resistance to white domination and for refusing to join the U.S. Army during the Vietnam War. Lebron James holds the record for all-time playoff points, is an activist for various causes including social justice, racial equality, revitalizing African American communities, and working with pioneers in improving the education of our youth.

You were only eight months, and you endured the drive to Clermont, Florida like a champ. Everyone knows traveling with an infant is a pressure on any parent. But you were different, you embraced the sixteen-hour drive. We stopped multiple times to feed you, change you, to stretch, and to rest. I wasn't thrilled about moving to Florida, except for, the warm weather and palm trees. I was the only child of my parents, and you were their first grandson. I came from a large family with many first cousins who were like brothers and sisters to me and many close friends with whom I shared lasting relationships that I left behind. Nevertheless, I was open to doing what was best for my family.

I stopped breastfeeding you and gave you whole milk. I was

12

concerned about how your body would digest the milk, but you took it like a trailblazer. As you began to grow, each day, I saw the young boy you were becoming. Even though you were shy and reserved, you were always approached by people who wanted to pick you up, hug you, and/or compliment you on how handsome you were. You were the child that everyone enjoyed being around because you were fun, loving, and no trouble.

You began to venture into sports at the age of eight. Baseball became your choice of sport. Your sister was and still is today your number one fan: always cheering you. We were elated to share with family and friends how you played and how proud we were of you, not just because you were my son and I thought you were the best player ever and never made mistakes. It was because you were young, and you hung in there and kept going.

Many nights I stayed up late washing your uniforms and those white pants that were soiled with clay. Your dad made sure you had the right baseball shoes, extra uniforms, the best baseball bats and gloves for your age, league, and skill level. It was a family hustle getting you together. We wanted to make sure you were prepared and felt loved and supported with everything you needed. You were young and you played with great tenacity. When you were by yourself in the dugout with your teammates, only God knew what was said; what you truly thought in your mind and felt in your heart.

I remember all your games, but one game always comes to my mind. At this game, there were more families than normal. There were so many people at the baseball field. You saw parents with siblings. I even noticed grandparents. There were multiple baseball teams present that day. This particular baseball game, I saw you on second base and then you stole third base. I could see from the side of your baseball helmet the expression on your face as you studied in preparation to steal home plate. From the looks of the spectators' faces, no one was expecting you to steal home plate, but their eyes were on you to get you out and not come home to score. You turned your head left, then right, and within a wink of an eye, you stole home plate. You slid into home plate and rose like the Brooklyn Bridge overlooking the city and the waves in the water. The umpire yelled "safe", and I could feel the negative energy from the doubters, haters, and naysayers as you scored a winning run for your team. I stood up like a victorious mom cheering you on and letting you see and others that I was proud of you. Physically you looked good, but I never asked you how you felt mentally that day. I just hated how the crowd responded. Jealous sneers, evil looks, and yelling he's not safe! However, your coach, team members, and other spectators supported you cheering for you.

Your name is characterized by the spirit of freedom, boldness, and independence. Throughout the negativity, you remained composed and determined to go for the win. I knew that you could accomplish anything when you put your mind to it. I saw your face and I knew the victory was yours. Regardless of the naysayers, you were still my champion.

Every Little League game you played you were the only Black boy on the team, and I noticed your sense of direction. The presence you exuded showed an attentive spirit, respectful demeanor, a team player. You were always a leader. I began to see an increase in favoritism as coaches allowed white players who, noticeably, weren't as talented as you to be able to play before you. The white privileged players advanced in the lineup. I knew only time would tell the true talent or the lack thereof from those players. You could overcome adversity and adapt. You were always dedicated to what you loved; others would view you as a champion, but you've always remained humble.

As you advanced on to high school, you were always selected to play varsity for the baseball team. Throughout your baseball seasons, you were selected to participate in various baseball tournaments at places such as Disney's Wide World of Sports Complex. You travelled with teams outside the State of Florida to various cities; played at the historic Dodgertown and was coached by professional baseball players. You attended three different high schools to prevail in the diversified realm of opportunities for a young Black baseball player. As your parents, we only wanted the best for you. Your accolades were endless. You were selected as the fastest runner; the team captain; the academically sound student; and the disciplined athlete that you, candidly, are. Not because we said it, it's because you were. I always instilled in you to stay prayerful and to always have a relationship with God. Always know, as your mother, I will believe you first, and no matter what; that you can always tell me the truth.

I remember vividly sitting in the stands watching you on first base getting ready to steal second base. With great anticipation, I could see the yearning in your eyes, like a hawk clocking its prey, as you crafted your lead off to second base. You got caught in a pickle and you twisted your body and dove back onto first base, and the umpire bellowed, "safe" from the deepest level of his lungs. As you stood up slowly from first base, with your back turned away from the crowd, I could see you raise your left hand and I was wondering why there was a pause in the game, when the referee had already declared you safe.

I felt you were taking too long to turn around to get back on base and even the fans in the stands noticed the pause and they were silent. Once you turned around to the crowd and held your left hand up, I knew something was wrong. You walked with your head high reflecting no pain and without hesitation, you walked off the field with your coaches toward the athlete trainers. This reminded me of how I carried you in the womb with pride and grace. But you, however, embellished the epitome of a great leader and was wise enough to make the right decision of when to leave the field.

As I left the stands, I jumped from a couple of steps onto the field where you were walking. I could see your left middle finger hung lifeless. I looked at you and covered my face with my hands, while my heart stopped a beat and my stomach ravished with agony. You looked at me with a smile and said, "Mommy, I'm good." Your father, coaches, and athletic trainers discussed snapping your finger back in place. At that time, I stepped away. I was already praying about getting ready to take you to the hospital. The coaches approached me and calmly said that you would be fine. We didn't take you to the hospital even though I felt that we should have to ensure you didn't have any bone damage. Your finger was wrapped for support, and you weren't in any pain. We went home that day, and all was good.

As I walked into the house, I could feel your energy as an artist at heart. I looked around our home and it reminded me of a gallery, because I saw your artwork on the wall from various school projects and vases throughout the rooms. I remember you were selected and nominated from your school for one of your drawings to be showcased in the county's community center. Today, I look at your left middle finger and thanked God for your finger because the circumstances could have been worse. For all that you are, you are always the champion of my heart.

The Last Lap

Now, it's your senior year of high school and I'm overjoyed. It's heartfelt to see how amazing you have grown over the years. I couldn't wait for you to experience a great senior year of high school as I did. I was thrilled that you could experience homecoming events and dances, despite briefly knowing if you wanted to attend. I dare to mention who you were going to take to the homecoming dance. That was top secret and to my surprise, you went solo. After you came home that night and shared the photos you took with your camera, it was evident that the night was a memorable fantasy, overflowing with laughter and happiness.

It reminded me of the time I was in high school and ran for homecoming queen and how I had a great time. To let you know, I went solo too! And don't ask me what happened when I got there. Your experience led me to reminisce on some everlasting moments of high school.

Before we could begin to think about another milestone of your senior year, we were hit with the nationwide virus, coronavirus. When this global pandemic was broadcasted through news and social media, I knew this would not only affect the class of 2020, but also shape the rest of your life. I was disappointed, knowing that this global pandemic had affected your opportunity to experience multiple milestones and memorable moments in your life from prom to most, importantly, graduation. Coronavirus came into our lives sweeping away all the memorable milestones that every mother and teenage child could ever dream. Surprisingly, these changes didn't faze you and you've adjusted to the privileges that this pandemic has deprived, and instead, began to embrace your new normal. Even so, your experience is a pivotal part of history, and your voice will speak volumes as to how you persevered through such life-changing circumstances and continued a successful journey to your first year in college.

Many times, I've been asked if I cried when I left you at college, but I did not shed one tear. My heart was filled with peace knowing that God will carry you beyond measure, continuously, like the love I have for you. That amid my fear of negative influences and experiences that this world may bring, I am proud that you have developed into a gratifying young man. No one else will ever know the love that I have for you, I have been gifted the love of my life for a lifetime.

Love Beyond Measure

This unique journey of yours is going to be tough. Despite our nation's discourse regarding the embrace of human diversity, Black males are still perpetually brutalized, killed, and negatively stereotyped. Recent occasions, regarding police killings, highlight the reality that even though Black males have the same constitutional and civil rights as all other citizens, in truth, their rights are often violated or denied. I fear how this world of injustice will create an environment and a negative perception of you. This world would dismiss your loving character and will instead classify you as a threat to society. My dear son, you are not what the world thinks, you are Maveric, uniquely, made from God. Ambitious, intelligent, caring, dedicated, and a great leader. The piece of my treasure that is loved.

Now, present-day I'm here and you're reading this love letter from me. You will have this letter from me for the rest of your life. I want you to know I love you beyond measure. I believe God presented to me, in this moment of my life, to be able to write this love letter and say these words to you without any doubt or fear.

I must let you know that mommy hasn't always been perfect. I have made mistakes. This life can't describe you. I'm your mother, but I'm not an angel. Some things should never be told, but believe me, I AM NOT PERFECT. I don't expect you to be perfect, I don't expect you to be an athlete.

I want you to grow and be happy with you. I always want the best for you. My wish is that you will be the greatest gift you can be for yourself. Be Happy. Grow. Love. Live. My wants are what every mother wants. I want you to know that this world, sports, and people don't define you. You can never disappoint me, because you are one of my greatest gifts. Of all the things that we can be, none is greater than the knowledge of self. Go out my dear son, to know who you are and why God brought you into the world and which of your attributes, from Him, equips you to serve the world.

CHAPTER 2

I LOVE THAT YOU ARE

BY MARIA MUHAMMAD

I LOVE THAT YOU ARE
BY MARIA MUHAMMAD

Dear Alif Muhammad, Jr. (affectionally known as Toot),

son, I thought I did everything right. In my eyes, I was the type of mother who invested in her children. I remember asking you before you decided on a college, "Toot, what is it that you want to become"? You told me you wanted to be a veterinarian. I replied, "Are you sure"? Based on your response, I planned a college tour, exclusively, for you and your closest friends. We visited five universities. I can still hear the laughter when you and your buddies realized that Morehouse was an all-boys school. When we toured Tuskegee, I knew this was the school you would choose.

The staff at Tuskegee exuded nothing but "Southern Hospitality"; they were wonderful. You really enjoyed touring the labs and meeting the professors. Your favorite tour was the veterinary hospital with the young doctors who were working on animals. This really got your attention. Your excitement about college made me so proud. My son was going to be a veterinarian. Education was my thing. If nothing else happened in my life, I wanted all my children to become degreed. I did not have that chance to go to college when I was your age. My son was attending an HBCU. He was attending "the prestigious" Tuskegee University. I was living my college aspirations, vicariously, through you and your college experiences. It was great.

Just like that, your first year of college became your third year of college. You were making a major life altering decision. You see, I never realized you were a man. In fact, I believe you realized it long before I did. To me you were my son, my child. If I had to pinpoint the moment you started stepping into your manhood; I would say it was when you got the news you were going to be a father. Oh, yeah! You were an adult, a man, no longer just my baby, but a Black man and a soon to be father. This was frightening. It was very frightening. I didn't feel you were ready to be a father.

Your reality was simple, you had a responsibility to the woman you would marry and the child you two would bare. I remember telling you that you don't want to stop going to college. You were attending the Tuskegee University and it was EXPENSIVE. *I loved that you loved animals and enjoyed nurturing them back to life.* Somehow, I thought this love would make you stay in school. All you had to do was finish your first four years. Then you would only have a few more years and you would be working in your field as a veterinarian. But when you found out that your girlfriend was with child, that was all she wrote. I am always wondering if you forgot the conversation we had about protection. This was not the birds and the bees. We really talked about sex.

Son, I was very forward with you during that conversation. Usually, fathers have conversations with their sons about sex. But your father didn't want to talk to you about sex, because he didn't want you to think that we condoned sex before marriage. I waited for the right time to have this discussion. My conversation with you was bold. I knew your dad didn't agree, but I had to have the talk with you. He didn't want me to even talk about condoms. So, I waited until your dad was away. You see, I didn't want you to come back home and have three, four, and five different girls pregnant.

Our conversation is just as vivid as yesterday. I said, "let me tell you something, you better be smart. When you look at a woman and you think you want to have sex with her, think about it. Son, if she is good enough to lay down and have sex with, she is good enough to be your wife. The one thing I will not tolerate is one, two, three, and four babies from different women. You have a name to uphold. With that alone, you carry yourself "properly". Then I gave you a huge box of condoms for your protection.

I was not giving you condoms, because I believed in sex before marriage. I was giving you condoms because I wanted you to be safe if you became curious. Honestly, son, I wanted you to exercise self-discipline and not bring home a bunch of babies from a bunch of "babies' mommas". That is why, I told you to wrap yourself up. Even in that moment, I always knew you would be a good father and provider. But I wanted your story to be different. I did not want you to approach this course of life in the wrong manner. I did not want you to have five or six children on your head. It was inevitable, you left Tuskegee to become a father and a provider.

My wishes were for you to stay the course your father and I put you on. When you began considering dropping out of school, it really hurt me. Because I remember the sparkle in your eyes when you saw the medical section of Tuskegee and learned about the animals. I knew this was the school for you and you would be successful. It was always my belief that if you acquired an education, you could dictate your own path. I wanted you to take your education; comeback to the community; set up a business and not have to work for a corporation. I wanted you to work for yourself; dictate how much money you were going to make; determine who you were going to hire; and when you wanted to take vacation.

What happened. We had one year left, and I would be participating in the Tuskegee tradition and watch you walk across the stage on Mother's Day! We wanted you to succeed. We wanted you to go to school and get a degree and follow your passion. We offered to raise and provide for your baby until your girlfriend finished college. But you were your own man. *I love that you are an independent thinker.* Your departure from college was your own journey. In your journey, you decided you were in love and the woman you impregnated would become your wife.

We instilled faith, strong values, and respect in you your entire life. But as you walked into this new path, I found myself giving you additional wisdom. I remember sharing with you to have respect for yourself. If you can respect yourself, you can respect others. I talked candidly with you about how to treat your wife. Yes, I said what most women say, give your wife the same respect you would give to your mother. I told you to never call your wife out of her name. I even went as far to say, that her mother and father gave her a name - so call her that one or a more loving name that you love to call her by. Honestly, son I really felt qualified to talk to you about marriage. I got married at 19 years of age. I knew that you would not raise your hand to hit a woman, but still I shared this wisdom with you. I wanted you to know that sometimes in marriage conversations can become heated and you might have to leave the room to remain respectful. We have had these mother and son chats all your life. *I love that you are very respectful of me as your mother, us as your parents, your grandparents, and all elders.*

Our mother and son talk became mother, son, and daughter-in-law conversations. Son, *I love that you are a family man. I love that you emulate your father's strong ways and will.* During one of our many conversations, I shared with you and your wife that the best teaching for your daughters and son was to keep your children in the mosque. Let them hear the Sunday lecture as a family. Put your daughters in the Muslim Girls Training (MGT) class. I said it shows them how to become a young woman. It shows them how to keep and how to take care of themselves, how to take care of their husbands, how to cook a meal, and how to sew. There are so many young women today who do not know how to cook. Some, because they were being educated, or they did not want to learn how to cook. This new generations believes fast food is good enough for them. Or that momma is going to have a meal ready for me, when I come home. But the reality is they must be taught how to be the best they can be. When we spoke that day, I said, "Son, keep them in the MGT class, everything you are teaching them about moral values and spiritual values, at home, will be reinforced by their Sunday lecture and their MGT class". It puts food for thought on their brain when they get ready to make a mistake.

It is now 2021, son you are a wonderful father, a wonderful provider, and a wonderful husband. I know your views about college. We've talked candidly about the debt, how expensive universities are, and I understand your mindset about college, and your responsibility to your family. ***Toot, I love that you are God Fearing. I love that God is first and then family.*** There is a part of me that still wants you to get that bachelor's degree, because you only have one year left. Something inside of me feels that it will free you up. Because if you decide you do not want to work for a large corporation or that you have had enough you will have your degree. In my eyes, these companies don't care about your well-being. I have always felt that you were just another employee or another number to the company. A degree could make you better equipped to leave your job and devote your time and energy to your own business. In my heart, I still feel you need to be a lettered man. That is what society is looking for and it would make your path a little easier.

My love for you is not contingent upon the things that I have wanted to happen in your life or that I would like to see happen. I love you for so many reasons. *I love that you're strong in faith. I love that you know how to persevere through hard times and good times. I love that you are entrepreneurial.*

So many years ago, you said you wanted to be a young parent like me, and your dad. Before, I could completely conceptualize you wanting to have a family, you knew you would have a wife. You had a complete plan for what type of parent you would be. You even knew what type of things you would do with your children. I love that you vacation with your family to broaden their scope. I love how you protect your wife and children. I love the way you love your wife and how you care for her in sickness and in health. I love that you give good advice about life to your daughters. I love how you coach and teach your daughters about young men. I love that you teach your children how to respect themselves and how they should be respected.

This year we were hit with one of the deadliest pandemics the world has ever experienced and through all the turmoil of life you remained steadfast. As we faced the pandemic, we did not forget our faith. During Ramadan, I was so honored to observe you leading our family in the five daily prayers [Fajr, Dhuhr, Asr, Maghrib, Isha'a]. When our family celebrated the Eid feast, I watched in admiration, your love for Islam; love for your family and how you continue to train your son and daughters. As we sat in the living room, distributing gifts, I remember your son's excitement when he received his Kufi and Kaftan robe. The atmosphere was full of love, the laughter of the young and old. Hearing your children call you dad was like listening to the sounds of a skilled violinist. It was music to my ears. In this moment, I saw you like I've never seen you before. Yes, you are a wonderful son, wonderful father, and wonderful provider. I saw your wisdom and your strength.

Throughout your life, I prayed that my son would help with the liberation of our people. I know that you are a warrior. God has a blessed me with a beautiful son. Don't sleep on your greatness. Put your feet on the path of the men that came before you and help them to liberate the masses of our people. You have the blood of great men running through your veins. Your blood is the blood of the Honorable Elijah Muhammad, the Honorable Minister Louis Farrakhan, Herbert Muhammad, and Imam Warith D. Mohammed.

But with the Grace and Mercy of Almighty God, Allah, like water you are destined to seek your own level as Allah continues to fill your life with His Mission. I must say, Son, without any doubt-your love, care, and provision of your family is very high on the list of examples.

Loving You Eternally,
Mom

CHAPTER 3

RESILIENCE

BY ALICIA COLE

RESILIENCE
BY ALICIA COLE

Flooded with instant replays of my life, observations from my childhood immediately revealed my mom as a powerful influence.

Before I became a mom, I was a daughter of a mom who taught me how to be a mom, even though she had no clue how to be one herself. WHEW! That was a mouthful; chew on that! My mom birthed me at the young and tender age of 16. She had to figure out how to parent really quick. Her and my grandmother didn't have the best relationship when she was a child. Instead, my mom turned to her godmother, who she deemed to be her saving grace, until her dying day. Thereafter, she relied upon her older sisters to help guide her along the road of becoming an adult and being a mom. Along that road my mom had a son and got married. For about fourteen years it was just the four of us and then two more daughters were born. I deem myself "the test dummy kid" in that, there were lots of firsts for both her and I! Whereas by the fourth child, my mom was pretty much well versed on raising her children; as the first-born child, I endured all the trials and errors a new mom had to go through. I think she did a pretty darn good job with the limited resources that she had. Hell, I think I came out pretty swell. From watching my mother's experience, I was taught what I believe to be one of the key components of being a mom: RESILIENCE. Let's explore that word for a moment.

RESILIENCE [ri-zil-yuhns, -zil-ee-uhns]
~ the ability of a person to adjust to or recover readily from illness, adversity, major life changes, etc. {Dictionary.com}

Now, let's get into my story as a mom and how resilience played its role throughout my experience of becoming a mother.

I am a big chicken when it comes to pain. I vowed that if I ever desired to be a mom, I would adopt. The thought of enduring the horror stories of excruciating pain that my female counterparts shared so willingly was more than I could imagine! Although children were not in my plans, life happened. I became pregnant in my early twenties (during my college days) and gave birth to a beautiful baby girl who is now a woman with children of her own (my Hunni-Babies!) However, seeing those childbearing horror stories come true, I was content with being a mom of an only child for the rest of my life. I did not foresee myself going through pregnancy ever again. As time went on, I married and my WAS-band (husband at the time) wanted to have a child, but I declined for five years. My WAS-band had two children of his own prior to our marriage and I had one child. I figured, we were good, and our family was complete. Unbeknownst to him, after a five-year span of saying no, I stopped taking birth control and yielded to the idea of bearing another child. This is very important, son, so pay attention.

The year was 2000, and I had just gone through a tumultuous health scare dealing with chronic sinusitis and meningitis. That is a book in and of itself. For the sake of this story, I'll flash forward to the day I was in the hospital about to undergo surgery to repair something internally that went terribly wrong in a previous surgery. Before anesthesia, I was asked the standard questions that

31

must be answered prior to administration. One being, "Is there any possibility that you could be pregnant?".

My WAS-band and I answered at the same time. Only, his answer was "no" and my answer was "yes". I smiled coyly and he gave a look of surprise. He was expecting a mutual answer. But remember, he had no clue that I had stopped birth control. I shared with him that I had acquiesced and would have his child.

Everyone needed sunglasses for the smile he gave. While the nurse stepped out of the room, he was still in shock and talked about how happy he was. The nurse returned with the anesthesiologist who shared some not so joyous news. I remember this as if it were yesterday. She told us that we needed to decide; due to my severe medical situation, either abort the child and proceed with the surgery, or go through with the pregnancy and risk dying. In an instant the room went dim. She said she would give us a little time to mull it over. We were left in that room for five minutes, but it felt like five seconds. We were flooded with emotions as we discussed the situation. I remember my was-band telling me "we can have a child again, but we can't replace you". Yet, as sweet, and genuine as that sounded, I could not bring myself to agree to that plan. When the nurse and anesthesiologist returned, I told them that I was going through with the repair surgery, and I was going to keep my baby.

I mentally prepared myself to deal with whatever the ramifications would be, including death. The seriousness of the matter was reiterated to me, and my WAS-band looked like a lost puppy, sad, and distraught. I was handed paperwork to sign stating that if it came down to saving me or the baby at the time of delivery to save my baby and let me die. I signed those papers with a smile, and they wheeled me into surgery. I was confident and excited to be carrying a new life inside of me. I had declined pregnancy for five whole years before deciding to have this bundle of joy and there was no way that I was going to let it go that easily.

RESILIENCE [ri-zil-yuhns, -zil-ee-uhns]
~ how much you want something and how much you are willing and able to overcome obstacles to get it. {dictionary.com}

My greatest blessings are the seeds that I bore. Each precious jewel that I was blessed to birth is unique in their very own fabulous way. I can write a chapter on each child of mine. However, this chapter is dedicated to you; My Black Son...

I must be honest; you came here rotten to the core! You were a screaming baby. I have delivery room memories of the day you were born. The nurses said they were taking you to the nursery after they got you all cleaned up and that I should try to get some rest. I sighed with relief and closed my eyes to nap. Well, that was short lived. There was a constant cry from a baby coming from down the hall that would not allow me to sleep. I had a feeling it was my baby boy. I pressed the nurse call button and the kind voice on the other end asked me if everything was, ok? I asked; "is that my son screaming like that for all that time?" She said, "yes, it is, but try to get some rest, he'll be fine". I told her that I could not rest with you screaming like that and to bring you to me. As soon as they wheeled you into my room (without me even touching you), you stopped crying. Talk about spoiled! Like I said, you came here rotten to the core!

For the first three years of your life, if anyone attempted to hold you, you would scream until you were in my arms again. I was an educator at the time and thought I would return to work and let your grandmother care for you in my absence (I was not quite ready to trust anyone outside of family). I called to check on you during my lunch break and there you were in the background just as loud as you wanted to be screaming. My mom felt helpless. I ended up taking an extended leave of absence to stay home with you. At home, my arms were your happy place. I couldn't handle chores without you on my hip nor take a shower or cook a meal. Your dad would have to fly you around like a superhero to keep you quiet until my arms were available again. You even screamed with him uncontrollably until he discovered that superhero trick as a temporary fix. Because I felt like it would help you to stop crying for me so much, I enrolled you into a daycare to be around other children. I thought this to be a great way for me to get back to working and for you to get used to being with others without me around. That too was short lived as that childcare facility threatened to put you out because you screamed at the top of your lungs from the time, I dropped you off until I picked you up. I thought for sure that I would be making the news as Chicago's next postpartum depression mom who jumped off of a building or something. You, my son, were completely attached to me and there was absolutely nothing we could do about it but to embrace it. I was certain that your newborn years of being a screaming, clingy, needy little boy were going to determine your next phases of youth into adulthood. How wrong I was.

RESILIENCE [ri-zil-yuhns, -zil-ee-uhns]
~ emotional strength

As soon as you began to talk, I knew immediately that you were going to be a special kid. From your very first words, you commanded authority. You were a serious kid with sarcastic humor and as you are today, you were always filled with an abundance of questions. You never settled for simple answers as your intellect would not allow you to. You spoke frankly and that, might I say, was challenging to deal with as those who did not know you would be in for quite the encounter. Ready for a chuckle? You were in the third grade, and I had just picked you up from school, so we were in the car. While driving along, we arrived at a four way stop. You asked; "Mom, how do the people know which car's turn it is to go?". With a smile of confidence, I gave you the best 3rd grade answer that I could give. You said "hmm" and turned to look out of the window. We rode along for a few more blocks in silence and out of the blue you said "Mom, according to the lines of symmetry that is incorrect". Well, blow me down! I'm talking to you with remedial words, and you hit me with "the lines of symmetry"! That along with many more instances to come was further confirmation of your beautiful mind.

My son, you are crafty, intelligent, and creative. You've always had the ability to come up with hustles. It seemed like every year you were doing something to get extra money for something that you wanted to buy. In the fifth grade you sketched pictures of your friends so that you could have dollars in your piggy bank. Seventh grade you said, "Ma, I researched this pet I would like to spend my money on. With everything that we need to care for it, it will cost us around $300". I gave you a blank stare thinking, you couldn't possibly have $300 in your bank (and you didn't). However, you were such a good kid, who rarely asked for anything, so it was hard for me to say no. You also sold candy to your friends from your locker to try to help with the cost. Ninth grade came and you charged kids to complete their extra credit homework. In eleventh grade, you were utilizing your saxophone for Prom-posals for a fee (yes, PROM-POSALS were a thing). For a prom-posal, someone would set up an extra romantic situation to ask their interest to accompany them to prom. You were on the high honor roll every single year from kindergarten to high school. You finished your Senior year graduating in the top 10 of your 300+ class with honors and a full scholarship to your choice HBCU.

A towering, medium complexioned; naturally curly-dark haired, intellectual musician you are. Over the years you've dealt with a vast number of adults and peers telling you that if you want to be successful, you need to play basketball. Without fail, anytime we were out, someone would ask what team you played for. I would brace myself each time because I knew sarcasm was coming. You would give them such an educational answer. They would stand there with the expression of "oops, maybe I shouldn't have asked that". You had no problem letting people know when they were being stereotypical. Your sarcasm and directness are pointed. It irritated us both when people would tell you that you were wasting your height not playing sports as if that was your only ticket to success. You were actually very good at every sport that you played. You just had no interest in joining any organized sports program and although I was a sports coach myself, I was not going to force you to join any team. You were more intrigued by what made things work and playing music. You were a wiz in every academic subject imaginable. You even aced the courses that you deemed too challenging. Even when you were in the fourth grade and was asked to select an instrument to play for music class, you chose an alto saxophone. The teacher said that you had to play a clarinet before you could play the saxophone. You refused, stating that you would learn the saxophone. We bought you a saxophone and with the guidance from your three great band directors (Christopher Smith - Primary School, Valeaka Freeman - High School, and Dr. Roosevelt Griffin - Griffin Institute of Music), you mastered that alto saxophone playing

36

genres of music from jazz, blues, classical, hip hop, marching tunes and more. You even self-taught yourself how to play four additional instruments.

Although the naysayers told you that you needed basketball to be successful, you persevered in what you love doing...figuring things out and playing music. You are a musician at heart and all three of your band directors saw that in you and helped me along the way to expose you to national opportunities. I am proud of your full ride scholarship to your selected university (Tennessee State University). I am proud of your chosen field of collegiate studies (Civil Engineering). I am proud of you being selected to participate in not one but three of your university bands. I am also proud that you are brave enough to conduct your very own band (The J. Cole Experiment).

RESILIENCE [ri-zil-yuhns, -zil-ee-uhns
~ To be able to spring back into shape after being thrown off your square

Before you were born, I was told that one of us wouldn't live should I go through with my pregnancy with you. Well, I did and here we both are so, how wrong were they? Resilience pulled me through and continues to keep me strong. Now, I see resilience in you Jamal Cole, my Black son. Thank you for your unconditional love. Thank you for your patience as I learned to be patient with you and all that you entail. Thank you for your uncomplaining heart that exudes kindness. Thank you for your frankness and your ability to speak your mind intelligently no matter what circumstance is present. From a baby boy to the young man that you are today; I pray that you continue to be genuine and do what makes your soul shine.

To all the Black sons out there, I say to you...Embrace who you are. Do not be afraid to stand for what you believe. Enjoy this thing called life because the naysayers will try to guide you to do what they think will make you happy. You are the pilot on your flight so set your goals high and crush them! While walking through the stages of life remember, YOU make your dreams happen; come through!

CHAPTER 4

Dear (a)MERICA, Let this Black Boy Live

BY DR. PAVIELLA FOSTER

Dear (a)MERICA, Let this Black Boy Live
BY DR. PAVIELLA FOSTER

Sincere, the perils of life will come as a Black boy and as a Black man, but no matter how many arise your Black mother will do her best to show you the joys of being Black. To my Black boy joy, you are necessary, you have the right to be loud, you have the right to smile, you have the right to breathe, you have the right to jog, and you have the right to LIVE. Anything used against you is not because of how beautiful you are, it is because of the power of your blackness.

The perils of this world have snatched the lives of so many Black boys and men. They have robbed the lives of so many beautiful Black people whose lives mattered. One day, my love, I will teach you of the times you live in. Although it saddens me, what brings me joy is that it ain't nothing like "Black boy magic." Now I lay me down to sleep, I pray the Lord, my Black son's soul to keep. And if I should die before I wake, let this Black boy LIVE to see another day.

I knew this day would come. I guess I never expected it to be so soon. I prayed for you, I waited for you, and God answered my prayers. As I write this love letter to you, Sincere, I am in awe of God and how blessed I am to have such an amazing and smart two-year-old. Before God showed me you, He challenged my thinking, my views, my thoughts, my fears, and my very being. During one of the darkest times of my life, God showed me His light: you. He knew I needed to be rescued, so he sent me his saving grace wrapped in two receiving blankets, an oversized infant hat, and the smallest sleeper. I accepted the most precious gift God could have ever given me, Sincere Jeremiah Coleman. You don't have my eyes, but you are my reflection. We don't share the same last name, but you are my legacy. My blood isn't running through your veins, but I know God has you covered in HIS. I could never express how much you mean to me verbally because at two years old, you wouldn't understand how you have saved my life. So, I hope that by the time you can read this love letter, your story would have saved so many other beautiful Black boys.

Dear Son,

I love you. I love you more than I have ever loved anything or anyone. You have been my light during so many dark days, my peace in so much confusion, and my smile during some of the lowest moments of my life. I write this letter to you not as an experienced mother but as a proud mother, a mother on a journey, a concerned mother, and a BLACK mother. As a Black mother I have to protect you from the scary monsters under your bed and the monsters clothed in white supremacy. My Black son, loving you is easy, but what's ahead scares me. One day, I will have to have "the talk" with you: don't run, keep your hands on the dashboard, give direction to everything you are doing, never reach for anything, don't wear a hoodie, and don't walk in groups. Shit, this scares me!

As I inhale all of those thoughts, I exhale the sentiments of knowing that the fight I fight today will produce life for you later. Sincere, understand that I will always do any and everything I can to show you your worth and what your Black body means to this world. I don't know yet what you will be like, but I know you will be great. If doctors had to compete with you, you've already mastered saving my life. If sports are your calling, you've played the hell out of me left and right. I mean, even at 2, you've put every move on me. No matter what you decide, just know your Black thoughts, your Black mind, and your Black body has already conquered it. As you grow, remember that God is first, and He will always be your first friend and confidant. Even when I am dead and gone, remember God is and will always be by your side. Find yourself in Him first, even before you think you have found you. Trust Him, lean on Him, and give Him you. Never stop praying, and never stop believing. Keep God in your heart and on your mind; He won't ever fail you. When I don't answer the phone, or I don't know the answer, God will always be your solution.

I know you've never thought I would share with the world that you were adopted, but families look different, you were just blessed to be peculiar. Being different sets you apart. The day I picked you up, I was so nervous because I never imagined you would be mine. The day your dad called, the tremble in his voice concerned me, but he knew he was making the best decision for you. He didn't want anyone to have to carry his responsibilities for him, but he wanted you to have a better life, because you deserve it. So, he swallowed his pride and asked if I could give you a better life than what he could offer. He reminds me every time we talk how he loves to see your smile and how much you have grown. The day I picked you up, your Nanna grilled me. She asked me all types of questions, it was clear she loved you. She looked me right in my eyes, with tears falling, and said "take care of my baby, I will always be his grandmother, but I need you to be his mommy." I gave your Nanna and your dad my word that you would never want for anything, and I would do my best to give you a life that was full of opportunities.

Sincere, you were everyone's pride and joy, it was like everyone saw something in you before you could even speak your first words or take your first steps. I thought to myself, how could I give to you what you had already given to so many people? How could I give you life when you had already made life so much more purposeful? Your smile brought so much joy to every room, and your presence alone made my hard days much easier. This wasn't an easy transition for me, but it was a necessary one. I remember the first night I picked you up I told your Granna I had no idea what I got myself into but that I would love you. She said to me, "if God told you to care for him that is your assignment, and to not let God down." I knew then that loving you and caring for you wasn't an option. It was my duty. Son, your story is different but so many other Black boys share this same story. Remember to always embrace your uniqueness and never let anyone or anything make you doubt your worth. As your mother, I never want you to be misled or misguided. Your life doesn't stop because I didn't birth you, you are still wanted, you are always loved, and you are worth living for. You were never a burden. You are loved and irreplaceable. Sincere, your life means more than you could ever know to so many people, but to me you are my world. Now, don't get me wrong Jeremiah, you have given me greys at just 33 years old, and have made me question if I was doing this mommy thang right, but at the end of every night when you kiss my cheek, hug my neck, and say "goodnight mommy I love you" every grey hair is worth it.

It takes a village to raise a child-- it wasn't meant for a mommy to parent alone. I don't always know what to do or even how to do it, so I lean on my family and friends for support. I have made mistakes, questioned myself as a mother, and cried many nights, but our village reminds me of just how strong I am every day. Son, there were some days that I didn't understand, and some days I had to truly trust God. When you were one, actually you had just turned one, you scared the hell out of me. Two months after taking your first steps, you broke your femur (by the way, you are super clumsy). Not even a month later, you were hospitalized in ICU for four days because you had two viruses attack your lungs, and you were unable to breathe. Those four days were the longest days of my life, but I refused to leave your side. It took Granna and Nanna to make me go home and bathe. Jeremiah, you scared me laying there with all those cords attached to you, but you built my trust in God. You took my faith to another level. To watch you barely breathe and bounce back in less than 48hrs, I knew God's Word would never fail. Jeremiah, you are truly my blessing, but not only have you blessed me, but you have also blessed those around you. Some of the most important people in my life have found value in their lives because of you. So, when you begin to doubt yourself or even question who you are, remember these words:

Sincere, I truly love you because you are a part of me. Your smile and personality are a beacon of light and hope for the world. Jeremiah, you are innocent, intelligent, and beautiful. I love you☐
   -Dad

Sincere, Nana loves you. You came into my life when I was in a broken space and filled my heart with love, happiness, and peace. You are my joy. Love you.
   -Nana

Dear Papa, the prince of my heart. Your entrance into this world was not only a birth, but a blessing. Sincere, you are love personified. ☐
   -Love, Auntie Angela

I love you, Sincere, because you are (sometimes) the only person who can put a smile on my face. I love you because you are my little angel. Sincere, you are the little brother that I always wanted and the answer to my prayers.

   -Love, Christian (god-sister)

   I love you Sincere (SweetFace) because you're such a beautiful ray of light. You're warm love on a cold day. I am beyond grateful that you, Paviella, have given me the opportunity to be a part of his life as his godmother. It was an honor then when you asked me to be a part of his life and still is such an honor. I love you, Sincere, because you're my SweetFace and no one can ever change or break that bond!

   -Love, Godmommy

My Dearest Beautiful Boy,

   I have often wondered about the boundaries of love; however, since you have come into my life, I'm so glad that such a boundary will never exist for me. You are the love that I carry in my heart. You are the root of my root, the bud of my bud, and the sky of my sky. There is nothing you can do or dream that I will not be here or there or care or bare with you! I carry you in my heart, my sacred heart, where my love abides for you, forever and always! And always means always!

   ♥YaYa

   I love you little guy; Sincere, you are a Sagittarius just like me. You love to have fun, and at your age, you know how to enjoy life. You are so smart and intelligent, and you love your family just like we love you.

   Love, Papa

   Sincere, aka "TT Man", I love you sooooo much baby boy! You are the life of our family! It has been a joy watching you grow into the brilliant guy that you are. Thank you for coming into

45

our lives, we needed you! You completed our family! I love you forever

Love, TT Mika

Sincere Jeremiah, you were about five weeks old when I first held you in my arms. From that day, I knew you belonged to our family. I fell in love with you. You became my Grandman, and I cannot see my life without you. You have brought such joy to our family. I love you with all my heart and I will always be your Granna.

-Love, Granna

Sincere, your kind heart and bright mind are noticeable whenever others share a room with you. Your random hugs are what I love the most, and you seem to always know when I need them.

-Love, Miss Johnson (head-start teacher)

Sincere,
You are a force of light, love, and courage. Your story has been beautifully written by the creator, so it is your duty to shine. I love you deeply, and I'm blessed to be a part of your village.

Love,
Auntie Moni

G-son, your skin is smooth like cocoa butter, your eyes are bright like the morning sun, and your smile lights up every dark room you enter. When you walk, it represents the KING you are. You walk with authority and confidence! You have swag, Godson, meaning you are Smart Wealthy Amazing and Gifted!!!!

-Love, ♥God-daddy

You are a wonderful little guy, sharing joy with that handsome smile of yours! You are full of great possibilities!

-Grammy

I love you, Sincere, because you felt like family the first day I saw you! Your smile is infectious. Your laugh is contagious. Your side-eye is dangerous. You know exactly who and what you want and when! This attribute will take you beyond the moon. I feel so blessed to see how God is navigating your footprints already!
-Dr. Tara Jenkins

What I like about you, Sincere, is that you are always playful, and you smile every time I mention sausage.
-Charles Jenkins, III

I love you, Sincere, because you are so smart and funny. You are very attentive and definitely a flirt. Your little eyes are so precious, and you don't have any fear at all. You are musically inclined and, just by looking at you Sincere, anyone can tell you can and will do anything you want in the world. I love how genius, loving, and wild you are. I love you, Sincere Jeremiahhhh

-Princess Jenkins □

I remember when your mom first mentioned you, she said "Reni, I need you to watch this baby for me for a bit while I'm at work." Little did she or I think that you would be our forever baby. Watching you grow from your first weeks to now has been such an amazing experience. You bring so much love and light into this family and this world! I never knew such a little body could carry and hold so much love within. You have shown us that love, Sincere, and I will always love you for it!
Love, TT Reni ("Ren")

Sincere, you are a piece to my heart that I didn't know existed. You showed up in our lives so unexpectedly and changed it forever. Your nickname is "Black Boy Joy", and it definitely defines you, because I can't help but to have joy when you are around.

-Love, TT Lena

Sincere, you exude joy!
You are not only a gift to your family, but you are a gift to anyone that enters your presence. Every time I have the chance to see you, Sincere, it warms my heart. My prayer is that God will continue to keep a hedge of protection around you, and the light of God will continue to shine through you.

-Love, Lady Bri

I love you, Sincere, because you breathe. You are a human being full of divinity deserving of a chance to make a beautiful life. I love the potential that I hear in your laughter, see in your walk, and feel when you smile. I love you because you are a mirror of me, a BLACK MAN, who will shine in spite of all the blistering darkness.

-Love, Pastor Sharpe

As I learn this mamma thang, hell, this human thang, know that you are my guiding light. No matter how many times I trip and fall, you remind me that accidents are inevitable. "Mommy, I'm ok, are you ok?" you said that often (lol). You and I are living in a time where things are beyond scary, unpredictable, and overwhelming; hopefully this letter helps you to ease your fears. So much has happened in just your 2.5 years of life. You are currently living through two national pandemics, one pandemic that has taken the lives of Black men and women at the hands of white supremacy. The other pandemic you are living through is called COVID-19, a virus that has killed over 100,000 Americans. When I learned about the COVID-19 pandemic, I feared that we would stay in the emergency room because you kept me there the first year of your life. I feared that your body couldn't handle being around others or being outside. I feared that your breathing would act up and send us back to ICU. So, I kept you in during 2020, and kid, when I tell you, you are strong and FEARLESS; you took every transition like a champ. When you had to stay with Granna, or be with Nanna, and then come home only on the weekends, you went with the flow. I knew it had to be hard not being in school and not seeing little people your own size, but trust that mommy did what was best. While one pandemic had me fearful for your health, the other had me fearful for your life as a Black man. I didn't know how to see Black men die and not see you. I didn't know how to see Black mothers weeping over caskets while white supremacists walked free and not think of myself. All I knew was that your smile was too precious to lose to *either pandemic*, and you needed to live to read this letter.

Although we are living in these unprecedented times, it won't always be like this. There will be times of peace and laughter. There will be times of joy and amazing moments because God has promised those things to us. When things become challenging, don't throw in the towel, ring it out, let it dry, and finish the fight. When folks see your differences, remind them that you were made in the image of God. When people judge Mommy because of who she chooses to love, remember that love covers all, and God has already fought that battle. Always remember, son, that you are fearfully and wonderfully made, and you are made in the image of an awesome and mighty God. When people challenge your thinking, show them that you can't be defeated. Always remember, you aren't a pretzel. You don't have to twist or turn to fit someone else's mold, and what's different makes you beautiful.

Living as a Black boy, teenager, and man will not be easy, but I promise that the person you are destined to be is worth every breath you take today. You will have to fight the perils of this sick world. You will have to do more and prove yourself more because you are BLACK. You will be tempted and challenged to lower your standards but remember to always stand tall. You will see and experience injustices but remain humble. One day you will carry many roles; you will be a brother, a friend, an uncle, a father, a husband, but always remember you will always be my son. You won't always make the best decision, Jeremiah, but I promise as your mother to provide you with the best tools and skills to live out your ancestors' faith. Don't ever conform, son, and don't ever stop fighting for what you believe in. Believe in your voice, believe in God, believe in yourself, and the power in being a Black man.

Love always and forever,
Your Black mamma!

 **5**

A MESSAGE TO THE PRESUMED FATHERLESS & MISGUIDED SON

BY OSEI HAWKINS

A MESSAGE TO THE PRESUMED
FATHERLESS & MISGUIDED SON
BY OSEI HAWKINS

Today I checked for mail. It didn't come today. But I'm sure it will come tomorrow. Again, this year, I was waiting for my birthday card. Broken promises. Promises of bicycles, motorcycles, cars, and visits. When I think about my dad, those are the first thoughts that come to mind. I was a son waiting for my dad to deliver on multiple promises. A son hoping for a Father who would just give him some of his time.

Early on, I would wait on him to call me on my birthday. Especially, when I had just reminded him when my birthday would be, the week prior. I would listen for the sound of the phone ring because I would expect him to call. It didn't happen.

As I grew into manhood, I stopped expecting anything from him. The life of broken promises had become normal. His words became like a soft wind, enough for me to hear, but not strong enough to create movement. But, what the heck, I still didn't give up on the possibility of his change and my desire for his time.

The last chance he had to deliver a broken promise to me was my wedding day. I invited him. He received a face-to-face invitation, and not only did he not attend, but he didn't call, no congratulations, nothing. I must admit, I was a little disappointed with this one. This was my attempt to welcome him into my adult life, since he wasn't there in my youth, but it was back to my normal.

When you're young, you look at your family in search for examples of what you could be. The aspiration of being a great father, family man, businessman, uncle, friend, homeowner, or any other growth challenge life could throw at you. For a young man, with no model into manhood, proper growth becomes challenging. My father was never there, and my uncles, aunts, and grandparents passed early in my life, so the wisdom that could have been passed on, never was. So, I hardly experienced an uncle/nephew relationship, or a son-to-father relationship.

So, everything that I know about being a father is based on not having one and wanting that love. All the paternal elements that I give to young kings and young soldiers is because of God. He put the right people in my life, allowed me to bump my head and grow out of whom I was to become to whom I was called to be.

Sons, I made myself a promise before you ever existed. My promise is that "I'm going to simply be there". The pain of not having a father present to love me, discipline me and teach me how to be a man is, forever, a part of my DNA. Loyalty, trustworthiness, and unconditional love - I have learned from my mother. While our stories about our dysfunctional fathers are similar, it wasn't her responsibility to teach me to be a man, but she mastered loving me and allowing me to grow. My mother had a family trait. She was an unrestricted giver, and it surpassed the people under our roof. If she had a yard, you had a yard. If she had a house, you had a house. It was of her character and practice that grew into my way of concern for others and realizing our connections to other human beings.

Before my biological sons were conceived, it wasn't uncommon for me to meet a brother on the street and embrace his struggle or his experience. When this started, I didn't know where God was taking me. I just felt a need to bond with other young men. In my eyes, a soldier is a fighter, and fighting is all he knows. He fights to win, no matter the cost, but when he realizes or is taught that he must grow into a king, his perspectives changes.

A king knows his strength, but, more importantly, he knows how and when to use it. He learns that winning the battle is not more important than winning the war. He understands there is a bigger picture that is bigger and more important than himself. He knows he should be honored and respected, but he understands he must give it as well. He understands that he is not only blessed, but he is and must be a blessing to others.

A king recognizes that he was first a soldier, because it is going to take some fighting to get to his destiny. A king must work hard to protect himself from the distractions that will detour him from God's purpose in his life. Prior to parenting, I volunteered my time to help young soldiers realize that the fight was not a physical fight. It was a fight to remain focused and driven. For each of these sons it was a fight with themselves.

Every king has an inner soldier; however, every soldier must know that he can be and must, continuously, strive into kingship. Don't get me wrong. You all have the potential, but knowledge, growth, and understanding are keys to your progress. Kingdoms are not just given to those who just stand up and claim it, but you must also prove yourself worthy of that leadership. Some situations will be put in a king's path to strip him of what God has promised him. The King and soldier is a perfect balancing act that is only present when you know whose you are, and who you are.

The world has many examples of soldiers who become great kings. Your battle in life may be like King David in the Bible. He came from server to soldier to king and he, continuously, had to fight. He was proclaimed to be king, but on his journey to becoming King he had to face many battles and he had to unleash his inner soldier.

After, officially, becoming the King, he still had to battle and work and sometimes avoid battles as he did with King Saul. He wasn't a perfect King. In his lifetime, he committed murder; he committed adultery; he was ruthless and numerous other things which were frowned upon. Through his entire process and his inner battle, he always maintained his relationship with God. He was successful because he continuously submitted to God. It's impossible to be a successful King without being subject to God.

David showed God he honored and respected him by never making the same mistake twice and God protected his son and covered him even when he was out of line.

Young King, young soldier you are the essence of greatness in the process of **becoming.** If you are wondering why I call you King, you must know and always remember who you are and from whence you come.

I call you soldier, because you will always have to fight to keep the focus on these truths. Throughout your lives there will be many who will try to convince you that you are other than what you are called to be. They will try to judge you by your mistakes, your challenges, or your family. You must fight the urge of complacency and the temptation to be like everyone else. Pursue your greatness because it is within you. The pursuit of greatness must always be in your coordinates of life, for it is the most direct path to learn yourself and find your purpose.

BECOMING: Processing Into Your Destiny

Becoming has different levels. Essentially, it is the acknowledgement that you're destined for something bigger and that you are embracing the path that leads you into it. This is something that grows, because you are not born knowing your destiny, although it's in you. Knowing you were birthed for something great, but not having clarity of that purpose will be trying; but God reveals in segments and in His own timing not yours. Remember, who you are subject to. You must know that where you are is just one of many steps, leading you into your predestined purpose.

It starts with mastering today. As you grow into yourself, you will face situations. These situations will be focused on many things in your life; maybe it is your job, your relationship, stress, pain, family or whatever it maybe. Young Soldier, you must master that day. This helps reveal who you are because it identifies your strengths and your weaknesses. Yes, every king has some weaknesses and the quicker you understand and accept that, the quicker you can turn it into a strength. In this **becoming** process it will identify what truly bothers you and prick your spirit. When your spirit is pricked by issues that don't seem to bother other people or you just don't have any resolve to deal with it, yet you still can't let it go, because it bothers you too much. This is God's way to nudge you back on track towards your purpose.

These are the problems that you are born to solve. Now, you are facing those problems that God has caused you to solve. They start with small things that you may view as insignificant, but these small things are the breadcrumbs that train and lead you through your growth. As you master these things, you begin to learn and develop passions that will be key to guiding you through life.

At one point in my life, I used to fight carrying the weight of my family. I was the only man, and I was the youngest. Sometimes, it appeared that nothing would get done until I did it. My life was full. I was working extremely hard in my business. Everybody was enjoying the fruits from my labor, but me. As I was faced with different family situations, I was charged with bringing the family together at certain times. In these moments, sometimes, the burden or frustration came in, because I was young and thought someone else should do it, but some things just bothered me. This was my "**becoming** the Black son, the soldier, the "man" and accepting my role in the family.

I was responsible for keeping my family together. As I started making faith moves, so did my family. I started going to church. Next, my mother started going to church. Once I stopped fighting what I felt someone else should do, it clicked within me, and I embraced my role within the family. That took away the stress, the weight, what I initially viewed as a burden, became a badge of honor and a blessing of something God anointed me to do.

Please know that the process of **becoming** is a lifelong event and a never-ending growing process. You won't see it to its completion, till you see God and He says, "Well Done My Good and Faithful Servant". But if we are learning on the way, God blesses us step-by-step.

At times, you want to speed up the process. I know I did and still do sometimes, but it's the voyage that makes it fun. Enjoy and celebrate each step, no matter how small it is. It's the little things that create the big picture, so let progress move on. Yes, little by little.

Young soldier as you are taking steps in your battle to become king, you will encounter challenges. Every challenge is a new situation that will guide you closer to your destiny. As you acknowledge that you are subject to God, realize that there are no coincidences. Whatever you're experiencing or challenged by has its purpose. I often refer to these as trials and mastering these trials will make you triumphant. The trials will vary, but you are prepared to be victorious. You must learn that your strength and lessons are all around you. Sometimes in your life and sometimes in the lives of others around you, but if you would pay attention, you will learn the keys you need to get you to the next level. It's all part of your process of being **becoming** who God has called you to be.

PURPOSE: The Reason Why God Created You

Young soldier, as you are reading this letter, I'm sure you know that we live in a great world that despite its greatness, it is full of problems and hardships for a young Black man. As a minority in this county, I will use a term in the Bible, "A Remnant" and if you search remnant in the Bible, you will see how a few can change the world. Jesus only used 12 and your name has a destiny associated with it. Will you cure cancer? Will you create the next technological advancement that will change the world? Will you be an educator? Will you teach people how to love? Will you inspire someone by the way you live or the words you speak? God created you in His image and after his likeness and HE was one, also. So never view a remnant as weak or lessor than, but strong and able to accomplish anything for in this is your strength.

Byron Allen is an example of a Black son who was a young foot soldier working toward the kingdom. His journey started like that of most soldiers. He was entry level in the entertainment industry. His start began as a teenage comedian. Then he began writing jokes for a man that was King in the entertainment industry. He wasn't defeated by someone else's success. He continued to press toward **becoming** a King himself. His journey including many fights, but his hardest battle was racism. He faced numerous challenges, but during challenges he purchased the Weather Channel. This wasn't something that was easy to accomplish for a Black son. In the year, that I am writing you this letter he settled a 20-billion-dollar lawsuit against Comcast. Like

David from the Bible, Byron Allen (A Remnant) defeated a giant on the road to **becoming** King. God led him to his purpose.

Young soldier as you work toward your kingship remember, family first. You can't save the world and neglect the ones around you. The first lesson to growth is realizing what your role is in your immediate family. We all have one and the sooner you find and embrace it, the sooner a wait can be lifted.

Only you know your true current state, but if you're reading these words in a place of depression, doubt, dysfunction, illness, hurt, or pain, understand that we go through stuff in general as a man. You are not alone, and other black sons have overcome this feeling. If you're in the midst of prejudice or injustice, other Black sons can relate. Hopefully, you are getting closer to a place of happiness and joy. No matter the mood, just know that as a Black son myself, I was and am you.

See life has a way of testing one's limits and, sometimes, bending us to a state of brokenness. We were never taught how to deal with pain or how to deal with loss. We were just broken. When we must face a situation which we are not in control of, whether it be molestation, illness, heartbreak, unemployment, or loss of a loved one we feel less than ourselves. Brokenness shows up in many forms varying from simple or as complex as being called a ni---r. It is a breaking. A break of the lens or your view of reality and it resembles a smack in the face. As young soldiers, we are not taught how to deal with these forms of attack, so you fight. Fighting with no strategy to get your desired outcome is foolish, to say the least, and not Kingly.

Be careful not to fall into depression. It might be fighting your inner self, your uncomfortable habits, or your addictions. But when you know that there is something that you are going to have to fight to become- who God calls you to be, you understand that every test is a step into purpose. So, the key is to learn how to fight it. You must know that there's a God bigger than you and will fight the battles you can't. It is in this state of mind that you must acknowledge and follow God. I am talking about Salvation; it is key to accessing the inner strength your creator placed in you. Once done, God will see you through every battle. Take comfort in knowing that God's got you. There's not a battle that you can't win, because God is with and in you. Each moment is teaching you something about yourself and about God.

When you are young, the entire world seems to be at your reach. We're taught we can be whoever, whatever we want to be with no restrictions, no biases, no racisms, and no unfairness. Do you remember when you were young, maybe Kindergarten or first grade, they asked, "What do you want to be when you grow up?" In my case, I really didn't know, so, I answered what was most common and expected, "Doctor, Lawyer, Astronaut, Basketball Player or President". The reality is I would have loved to do any of these jobs. Honestly, I was clueless of what people with these jobs really did. I just knew that they had important titles.

No one really knew what they wanted to be. We often desire to be what we see. If our parents or favorite television character was a doctor, we aspired to follow their path. If our idol was a basketball player, we wanted to reach that status. Our thoughts are if they can do it, I can do it.

The realness of life is that everyone has a purpose. There is a route to your destination, which means there are turns you will need to make. There are people you need to meet. There are things you must go through. You will have some victories and some defeats as you work towards your kingship.

You can't focus on who is not present in your life. You cannot focus on what career choice your parent or guardians have or don't have. The focus shouldn't be on what material things you've acquired or what someone else has acquired. It's not about new shoes and designer clothes.

In moving from a soldier to a king you must take the following steps:

Step 1:   Be able to stand alone and not follow the crowd. You must be comfortable with yourself and your own decision.

Step 2:   Acknowledging that there is a God that is directing you.

Step 3:   Being obedient to God's word. The Bible is your guide to being obedient.

Step 4:   Master each moment.

In the Bible, the scripture James 1:4 sums up how to get from being a soldier to a king. The scripture says, "Let perseverance finish its work so that you may be mature and complete, not lacking anything". Sons, I am sharing this scripture with you, because you must go through the process.

We are all subject to a Higher Power whether acknowledged or not. You will know that you are a king when you can stand alone, and you have reached maturity. God gives us our talents and skills. When must understand Ephesians 2:10, "We are God's Masterpiece," created in Christ Jesus to do good works, which God prepared in advance for us to do. We can't use them for wrong. If your talent is being able to talk, then attract or convince others.

You cannot use this talent for evil or destruction. If your talent is in finance and money management, you can't use it to schemes to rob the people or illicit ploys to disenfranchise or rip them of their life savings. Master your moment soldier and grow into your Kingship.

CHAPTER 6

THROUGH THE TEARING OF DIVORCE

BY FREDA SOWELL

THROUGH THE TEARING OF DIVORCE
BY FREDA SOWELL

Love recognizes no barriers. It jumps hurdles, leaps fences,
penetrates walls to arrive at its destination full of hope.
~ Maya Angelou

My Three Kings,

You are the reason I want to breathe every day. You are the reason I want to be a better person. You are the reason my world exists. The moment you arrived into this world, and I looked into your eyes, I saw a pure love, an innocent uncontaminated love that I wanted to protect from the wilds of this world. I want you to know that you matter, your vision on life matters, and standing on what you believe matters. Although life will bring blows and knock you down so hard that you may feel there is no way to get back up, always remember who you are: A KING, A RULER, AN OVERCOMER, A MAN OF WISDOM, A MAN OF ABUNDANCE IN WEALTH, AND LOVE. You are one of a kind, and no one can be you. Watching you become men has taught me to appreciate life and appreciate you. You have encouraged me to look within myself and ask, "What can I do to be a better woman and mother?" I want you to always know you are the apple of my eye. Your pain is my pain, your joy is my joy, and your love is my love. You not only put a sparkle in my eye, but in the eye of everyone that you meet. Your presence lights up the room, and your words are catalysts for change. As you embark on your life's endeavors, understand you are not standing alone. You have God to guide you, my love to encourage you, and a strength inside of you that will change the world.

Who can define a mother's love? You can ask 100 mothers and you will have 100 different definitions. A mother's love cannot be defined with one single definition. It is the love of a child that gives a mother life, a reason to live, and a reason to matter in this world. A mother's actions are made without considering the pain or sacrifices she may have to make. It is her love that keeps giving when she feels she has nothing left to give. Is there ever a moment where a mother can say, "enough", "I am tired", "not today"? Never! It is the love of a mother that holds her family together the best way she knows how. But in the midst of all of that, mothers are not perfect. They can become broken. A brokenness that goes down to the depths of her soul.

One morning, I was standing in front of the mirror and saw I was almost 300 pounds. My face was tired, there was no life in my eyes anymore, and my whole body was hurting. Tears began to run down my face. I was disappointed in myself. "You look a mess, Freda!" I said to myself. It was at that moment I realized I had to come first. I was drowning mentally and physically, and I needed help. Everything seemed to rest on my shoulders. I never felt loved or appreciated, and it was too much for my mind and body to handle. The only way for me to free myself from this unhealthy environment was to pack up everything and get the hell out! But then I thought about the three of you. *What in the hell am I going to do?* Fear gripped me, all I wanted to do was stay and deal with the heartache for the rest of my life for your sake. However, I chose the side of courage; and relocated to another state. I was happy to start a new life for us. Even though you were open to going with me, my fear was that once you realized your father was not coming, you would rebel or go down the road of destruction. My goal was to nourish every area you would allow me to, so you would not abort your purpose. God set me on a journey of healing through loving you during a difficult time in our life. We went through many emotional phases: loving and accepting the fact your father will not be present, learning how to overcome your pain of separation, dealing with my own personal hurt of being divorced, and raising boys as a single parent. My hope was by continuing to love you and affirm my love for you, that would lead you to become the men I knew you could be. I did not just choose to relocate... I also chose divorce. Divorce!

What about the three of you? I have strong sons with hearts of love, compassion, and a strength you do not even know existed. God showed me how to love you by not focusing on the current circumstance, but what I could see in your future. I may never know the depth of your pain John Jr., Jeremiah, and Joshua. There were nights when I would stand at your bedroom door and ask God to please help me get through this dark time in our life. I did not want to lose your heart towards me. I was hoping that you would understand why leaving your father was best for our family. The emotional distance from you was torture for me. I wanted to help each of you push through the pain by keeping your focus on your education, being responsible and remaining accountable to commitments.

John Jr., Jeremiah, and Joshua, I come from a family of divorce, and my hope is that you will never have to go through the heartbreak of such a decision. Understand that every choice you make will come with a set of consequences, good or bad. So, choose wisely, know what you want and who you are when you decide to choose a life partner. Did I make a bad decision? No. The love I have for your father is a love that will always reside in my heart. Unfortunately, some marital traumas are only healed through divorce. I lost my identity. I forgot who I was. I lost my sense of purpose. I needed the freedom to find and love myself again while at the same time trying to be the mother you needed.

John Jr., spending time with you during your swimming events or talking about a class you wanted to receive an A in, gave us a moment to connect. There were moments where you doubted yourself, the frustrations you were dealing with each time you stepped on the starting block, and the time when you did not receive what you expected academically after putting in so much work. I wanted to make sure you knew I was your biggest cheerleader. Whether you won the swim event or received an A on an exam, I got you!

Jeremiah, my greatest joy was being there to support you at every game, being a part of your football world allowed me to feel close to you. I wanted you to let me in your heart and tell me about the pain you were feeling. There were times you and I would sit in my room or on the patio and share what was going on in your life; that gave me hope that you were still with me. I knew I could not take the pain away, so being available to listen and affirm your strengths and hopes you had within yourself was my joy.

Joshua, my greatest disappointment was when soccer was over. We moved during that time, so you had nothing to identify with that felt like home. It was painful for me knowing you had to figure out how to fit in with your peers. I saw your frustration, and I am so sorry. No matter how I tried to explain how sorry I was, the distance between us increased. Whatever it took to make you happy, I did it. I would give and let you do whatever because I felt I owed you. I spoiled you. If that is what I needed to do to have a presence in your life I did it. ***If the boys could only understand***

what I was going through, maybe they would be more merciful.
But to no avail, my prayers were going unanswered.

I was angry because there was no reciprocity. I was lonely from the emotional distance I felt with each one of you. I felt abandoned because I wanted you to understand it was hard for me, too. I felt alone throughout this whole process, and my sister was my only place of refuge. She listened to my heart, prayed with me, and gave me words of encouragement that kept me focused on doing what was in your best interest. There was always a tap on my heart telling me to keep trying to make it work. You three were my miracles, and that alone made me want to give you the best of myself. But even when I felt that I gave everything from my heart, there was still a cloud of pain that swallowed that speck of goodness. When I made the decision to get a divorce, all kinds of emotions ran through my mind: the devastation of you not living with your father, questioning my actions, and trusting my decision to take care of you. Divorce is not something that I took lightly we were married for 18 years. It was the most difficult decision I ever had to make. Although I was dealing with my own emotions, I had to figure out how I would make your world a safe, peaceful, and productive environment. All I knew to do was pray and ask God to show me how to change the circumstances in my life.

Growing up in the church, I believed God would make everything okay. I believed things would get better, and life would be bliss. No matter how much I prayed, fasted, or sought counsel, God never showed up in the way I needed him to. It only got worse. Although a subtle peace resided on the inside, it was not enough to keep me from crying every night. I was an emotional reck, trying to hold it together. As time continued to progress, I could see how the separation began to affect you, the anger began to unravel - always testing me with disrespect and rebellion. I had to try to understand that you were hurt and confused.

John Jr., I remember you asked, "Mom, can you and dad start over and not let us be another statistic? I don't want to be a child of divorce." I understood how much it hurt for us to not be together as a family. Sometimes, life decisions will bring pain that we can't understand, but it is for the best. We must find a way to press through the pain by focusing on God's purpose for our family.

Joshua, thinking back to your transition as a teenager, I can see how dealing with fitting in, moving to a new home, and going to a new school was upsetting and unfair. My hope lied in your personality and ability to make new friends. Although your words were sharp and painful. I felt your pain and frustration, I stayed available to help talk and comfort you through the challenges you faced.

Jeremiah, your words were like bullets to my heart. The assertiveness was more than I could handle., "There is no male presence." "We must listen to a woman to help us become a man." Wow! I swallowed my words of anger and tried to understand that those words were coming from a place of hurt and selfishness.

How can I help you understand how to be a young man? Jeremiah, you were right. A mother can only be a mother, not a father. Although you could call him, not having him present is an emotion I can relate to. Being raised without a father's presence was my greatest pain. Although I could call him, I needed to feel his touch, hold me when I was scared and look into my eyes and give me a word of encouragement. I asked God for mentors for you. I reached out to your coaches, school counselors, and the parents of your friends to support me with keeping you on track. I knew and understood that there were gaps that I could not fill.

Throughout all the pain, I did not stop loving you. I tried to show you how much I loved you.

Divorce was not what I expected. My love for all three of you continued to guide and direct you in a path of success. I was always thinking of how to give you my best; however, without understanding how the relocation and separation was affecting you, I became very insecure as a mother when I needed to talk to each of you. My emotions were unsettling. I did not know what to do or say. I felt as if I was on pins and needles with you, only talking to you when I had to make sure your needs were met. The ability to have a conversation with you after relocating made telling you about the divorce even more burdensome. I did not want you to experience life raised by a single parent. I knew what that felt like - it's my story, too. It's a story I never thought would be my reality. A single parent raising three teenagers, what was I thinking? I was thinking it was the right thing to do for me.

Where is Christ in all this madness? Where is the Church? We have always been Christ-centered, and we still are. However, when I consulted with the elders of the church, I would get this kind of advice: "God blessed you with that husband, so you better do what you have to do to make it work." "God does not bless divorce." "Who is going to help you raise those boys, you cannot do it on your own?" All this advice kept me in the mental bondage of accepting my pain as if God gave it to me to live with.

John, you asked me if I believed in Jesus, and I said yes, but deep inside, I questioned how Jesus was taught to me, not my faith in God. All of the crying and begging to have my situation change was to no avail. It gave me more pain and confusion. ***Why would God want me so unhappy?*** I asked myself repeatedly all the advice I received left me questioning God's love for me. Why would a God so great stop loving me? I questioned everything:

70

why would God not want me to have peace, love, joy, and prosperity for my family? One day I was sitting on the patio crying out to God to help me understand why I felt this way. I heard God say, "I am not a God of rules, but a God of love." That moment freed me from the rules I was programmed to follow for so many years.

I decided to no longer attend church, and once I told you, the judgment I felt from all three of you made me feel unworthy to be your mom. I did not realize that all these years I was living in bondage to a message that does not allow me the freedom to be myself and love freely like God does. I found peace with that understanding hoping you see God's love through me.

My sons, as I pour my heart out to you, I can feel the sun shining on my heart again. I feel the healing and the freedom to do, be, and have anything I desire without the feeling of losing you. I am not the same woman or mother you saw as a child. I am better, stronger, and wiser with a love for you that far exceeds any circumstance you may face. We cannot go back and change the past, but we can definitely learn from it.

John Jr., Jeremiah, and Joshua, I leave you with this: although the pain made me feel like I had failed myself and our family, I am confident in the love you have for me. I may not ever understand how the tearing of our family deeply affected you, but I hope that one day you can understand how my love for you will never change. My desire is to always give each one of you the absolute best version of myself. And no matter where I am, my heart's desire is that you will always be able to hear my voice when you need an encouraging word.

A mother's love is stronger than distance, more powerful than time, and can transcend the grave. ~Tyler Perry

CHAPTER 7

LET YOUR LIGHT SHINE – YOU WERE BORN TO SPARKLE

BY LAQUITA MAXEY

LET YOUR LIGHT SHINE – YOU WERE BORN TO SPARKLE
BY LAQUITA MAXEY

This letter is my written expression of my love for you both and how special you are to me, some life's advice, and a reminder that you are an asset to this world. It saddens me that we still live in a racially charged America. We had to teach you the unwritten rules to keep yourselves safe as Black males in this world. I want you both to know that you are fearfully and wonderfully made by God. Your Black lives matter.

"My love for you is like tears from the stars. Mama." ~ Boyz II Men

Dear sons,

To our, handsome, chocolate drops that God created for a purpose and a bright destiny, always remember what God says about you. "Before I formed thee in the belly I knew thee; and before thou camest forth out of the womb I sanctified thee, and I ordained thee a prophet unto the nations." (Jeremiah 1:5) You are men of dignity, brilliance, and elegance. You are full of God's grace and your light inspires.

You both are my heartbeats. You are my sunshine and my dream come true. God chose you both and ordained me to be your mama; it was love at first sight. I'm forever grateful that I was chosen to be with you when you took your first breath. There was an instant bond. That twinkle in your eyes was mesmerizing. Your beautiful brown skin and your infant fragrance of cocoa butter was captivating. The moment I held each of you in my arms, I knew the labor pains and the long pregnancy were all worth it. Your dad and I are blessed to raise two kings. *"But ye are a chosen generation, a royal priesthood, a holy nation, a peculiar people; that ye should shew forth the praises of him who hath called you out of darkness into his marvelous light." (1 Peter 2:9)*

Sons, you are no longer boys but fine young men. I'm proud of who you are becoming. You both brighten my days and I'm grateful to share life with you. You are a light in this world with amazing destiny ahead of you. "Son shine" in the urban dictionary is defined as" a boy who is an actual ray of sunshine that must be protected at all costs." You both are protected and covered by the love of Christ. As a child, my Grandma Collins often sang this song to me "This little light of mine, I'm going to let it shine," and I say to you both, let your light shine. Sons, Shine!

Real Love

"Love is patient and kind. Love is not jealous or boastful or proud or rude. It does not demand its own way. It is not irritable, and it keeps no record of being wronged. It does not rejoice about injustice but rejoices whenever the truth wins out. Love never gives up, never loses faith, is always hopeful, and endures through every circumstance." (I Corinthians 13: 4-7)

Remember that God loved you first and real love comes from God. God loves you so much that He created you before the foundation of this world. His love burns bright for you and is unconditional. Always focus on God's truth: He loves you no

75

matter what, He is your comforter, way maker, and promise keeper. God will supply all your needs and give you the desires of your heart.   God provides peace that your mind cannot comprehend. I'm a living witness to God's truth, so trust God and embrace his love for you.

My love for you both started at conception. As your mom I will always love you with no strings attached. I will love you both for who you are and you don't have to work to earn my love. I will be your cheerleader as you navigate this journey of life. I will always support and advocate for you. I will push you out of your comfort to the greatness zone that God has for you. Know that with love also comes correction.

When I was in my 20s, I felt a love void in my life that I tried to fill with guys, material things, night clubs, and everything else the world can offer. I thought the void would go away after I obtained my dream of graduating from college or buying that new candy apple red Chevy Cavalier. None of those things filled my void until I turned my heart back to Jesus and developed a personal relationship with Him. That is where I found real love and received my daily strength. I learned that I was an imperfect person who makes mistakes, but God still loves me. Empty places in my heart were designed to be filled by God and not people, possessions, or accomplishments.

Always remember to love yourself. Be you, be genuine, be humble, and be kind to yourselves and others. No person, or thing can fill a void but God. Don't be consumed with the societal and media images of love because that is fake news. Don't listen to the negative inner critic but build on your strengths. When you look at the man in the mirror, see how handsome you are, but also go deeper and look inside to self-reflect and see your big heart, brilliance, compassion, and creativity. Get to know your real self from the inside out. Embrace your resilience, personality and purpose that are unique to you both. May you both continue to shine as the star that you are.

My love for you will not go away. You both are my chocolate drops and rays of sunshine. I'm thankful to God for blessing me with our Maxey guys. My fine, tall, strong, young men have outgrown my lap, but never my love. I made parenting mistakes at times. I may have pushed you too hard or did not push you hard enough. You don't have to earn my love. I apologize for times that I have judged you and perhaps made you feel that you had to think just like me. Forgive me for not listening more. My love for you both is unconditional, and I accept you both for who you are. Become the best version of you. Be the light this world needs. I will always love you. Remember that nothing you do will change God's love for you. God will always love you and so will I. Sons-Shine!

Greatness is in your DNA

Slavery in American tore families apart, couples could not legally marry, parents and their children were sold to different slave plantations. My family was intentional about connecting me to our extended family and upholding the values, roots, culture, and traditions. I cherish all the family gatherings, and reunions as it built strong bonds among generations. Knowing your family and your roots can help you appreciate how far your family has come.

You both come from an ancestry of royalty and greatness. "God saw everything that he made and indeed it was very good." (Genesis 1:31). Your ancestors worked hard, endured life's challenges and did not give up because they had you in mind. You come from a family of love and resilience. Our family members have prevailed over some of life's peaks and valleys in this world. Our family has overcome poverty, racism, addictions, abuse, mental illness, and health challenges.

However, I want to remind you that you come from a legacy of professionals that worked hard. You come from a family that worked in the cotton fields, a long line of educators, entrepreneurs, athletes, telecommunicators, and retail workers. We have family that have worked in medicine, automotive, law, and many with great culinary skills. Your profession is one way to carry out your gifts and talents, but never let it define you. You are special regardless of your profession. Shine on and sparkle, even if others throw shade.

As a child I was blessed with parents and extended family that poured love and encouragement into me. They pushed me to overcome life's challenges and trust God. My parents grew up in the south and migrated to Ohio when they were teens. My parents worked hard so that I can have a better future. I grew up in a very small two-bedroom home that was full of love (but not perfect) in Cleveland, Ohio. I was raised by my mom and stepdad with siblings Jermaine and Raushena. Justin came along when I was nineteen years old; I was in college at that time. Also blessed with my biological dad, James Roach, and siblings Michael & Lauren. Learn as much as you can about your family history, embrace our wonderful culture as this will help you unfold and understand who you are because greatness is in your DNA. Always listen and learn from the good and the bad experiences in life. Take the time to stay in contact with your family.

You all were blessed to have met and known not only your grandparents but multiple generations down to your great great grandmother, and to that I say you are blessed. As a family we endured a lot of grief and loss of life and we must say their names as a tribute: your great Grandma Collins, great Grandma Archie, great great Grandma Jenkins, Auntie Hallie, and your man and granddad - Pa Pa Maxey. In 2018 and 2019 we lost your two uncles Fritz and Tony and beloved Granny Granny Norma. You are a part of your ancestors' love, hopes, dreams, aspirations, and prayers. "Bringing the gifts that my ancestors gave, I am the dream and the hope of the slave. I Rise. I Rise. I Rise." -Maya Angelou

Nathaniel – Electrifying Light

You were our first-born son – my son shine. I became pregnant with you much sooner than I had planned. Fourteen months after the birth of Jennie-Lee you were in my arms and it was love at first sight. I remember holding you in my arms and staring at the beautiful sparkle in your eyes. You were always a curious child and had a hunger for learning. Continue to work hard, put time in, and work toward greatness.

From the time you were in middle school you expressed your interest in the medical field. You had and still have a gift for math and science. You are a trailblazer and will become a world contributor to something big needed in this world. Always remember this truth - you are chosen, you are a gift, you are a bright light in each day. You are highly favored by God, accepted, and radiant. You are my afro-sheen, sparkleberry Kool-Aid, and beacon of hope.

Growing into a young adult, our relationship has evolved where we can have real conversations about life. I will continue to work on being transparent about my past, present, and future. We won't always agree, but we must learn to listen and to be respectful. Always live out values such as honesty, integrity, faith, justice, compassion, generosity, and forgiveness.

Nate, accept God's unconditional love for you, and trust God to heal any brokenness. Unresolved brokenness will spill over into other areas of our lives if not addressed. Know that professional counseling and therapy is good for the soul. I have learned that my issues in life do not define me but build strength and resilience. Problems can become apart of our life's work. Don't let the dark shadows of your past define you, but instead use them as an opportunity to let your light inspire others. I love you – Son-Shine.

Matthew - Sparkles of Joy

I was pregnant with you when we moved to Indianapolis. We knew very few people in Indianapolis, and this was my first time ever living away from my extended family. I did not realize the impact this type of stress would have on my life. During my pregnancy with you, I developed issues with high blood pressure and was diagnosed with preeclampsia. I went for my doctor's visit, and she shared that you would have to be delivered almost six weeks early because my blood pressure was too high – YIKES.

You were created to win this race in life. You are a champion and a world changer. You are a light that shines bright like a sweet-smelling candle. Your siblings call you baby Matthew, as you are the youngest. Your dad and I call you our miracle child. You were so excited to meet your family you decided to come into this world early weighing 3.5 pounds. You were in the intensive care unit for two weeks, but I knew you were strong, a fighter, and a determined person, ready for the world.

You are smart, caring, easy going, and did I say handsome. You are the jokester in the family. You have an entrepreneur mindset, be your unique self and never try to conform to someone's image of you. In high school you received the diagnosis of attention deficit disorder, but never let that define you. Stay committed, master your craft and seek what sparks the light in you. I want to encourage you to stay focused on your goals and dreams. Don't let fear stop you. Push yourself to greatness. Your ideas are born in your uniqueness. Your dreams that you share with me are amazing, and I encourage you to embrace your greatness and strength.

You are my basketball guy. You can eat, drink, and sleep basketball. I love the dedication you put into the game of basketball, and I know it will be a big part of your future. I enjoy attending your games and watching your leadership on the court. Always, put the work in and make those dreams a reality. Yes, it will be hard. Yes, you will be challenged. Don't be afraid of success. Be a good steward of the greatness that God has placed inside of you. Be brave, be focused, continue to be a leader, and shine like beautiful Christmas lights. I love you. Son-shine.

Sunshine on a cloudy day

Opportunities can be created from life's challenges, something that we will face. In my fifty years of life, I have experienced a lot of trauma, but by the grace of God, I'm still here. While in graduate school I became pregnant and decided to have an abortion. For years I lived in shame, hurt, and regret over my decision. It took about twelve years for me to be delivered and truly receive God's forgiveness. I used this adversity to help other women who have had abortions; I'm finishing a book with stories of women and men sharing about their healing journey after abortion. I allowed God to use my pain as a part of my mission in life's work.

2010 was another challenging year for me. One of my dear friends, Tonya, was murdered by her husband. A month later your dad had a stroke and brain surgery. Life as we knew it drastically changed and we all had to shift to our new normal. While going through life's trials, I leaned into God's strength.

It was my faith that pulled me through. Adding the icing on the cake, we all endured in January 2018 your dad surviving a second stroke. This was a lot for your young lives but remember to cherish the memories.

Mom's Life Lessons

Sons, I want to give you some life lessons as you grow and further mature into adulthood. Love yourself by maintaining your physical and mental health. A gift you can give yourselves for your birthday is to have an annual physical and dental check-up every six months. Know your family's health history on both sides of the family. I love the fact that you both are physically active and stay on the basketball court and/or in the gym. Always stay active and let exercise be a part of your life. Get a good night's sleep and take naps when you can. Eat a healthy diet (yes, that includes fruits and veggies). In life we must maintain balance, so it is okay to eat that burger and fries sometimes, just not every day. Caring for your health and wellbeing is a part of loving yourself. Remember that what we put in our bodies at a young age can impact our future. Taking care of your mental health is equally important. I have sought the help from counselors and therapists, and it has been helpful. There is a stigma for males as it relates to caring for your health and mental well-being. Don't believe the lie that it is a sign of weakness. Having trusted family and friends that you can talk to can also be helpful, but don't let this be a substitute to seeking a professional therapist. Your health matters.

Keep Your Money Straight

Finances and money management is important to me, and I want you to be good stewards of your finances. Set a budget outlining all your expenses. Remember, your needs should come before your wants. As a college student, I made the mistake of getting too many credit cards and getting into credit card debt. While I paid my bills on time and built a good credit score stay away from credit card debt. I also spent a lot of unnecessary money shopping for clothes. I want to encourage you to break the cycle of poverty and learn to build wealth for you, your family, and our community. Spend your money on things that will gain value in the future: real estate, education, investments, and retirement savings Build on your gift and talents and develop multiple income streams. Budget your money and prioritize your spending on needs such as housing, transportation, utilities, food, and insurance.

Things to avoid
- Payday loans
- Debt
- Late charges, ATM fees, banking overdraft fees, etc.
- Living on student loans
- Co -signing on loans
- No such thing as a get rich quick scheme or fast money that is legit

Things to do

- Work hard in high school and college and keep your grade point average 3.0 or higher. This will open the doors for academic scholarships and that means no or less student loan debt.
- Live on a budget. Know where your money goes. Pay yourself a weekly allowance.
- Develop and keep a good credit store. When you have a good credit score you can keep more of your money rather than spending it on higher fees.
- Have an emergency fund. Save and plan for big picture items.
- Save for your future - Start saving for retirement in your early 20's and don't touch it.
- Pay your taxes.
- Have multiple income streams.

Find Out What Sparks The Light In You

My chocolate drops always remember that you are loved. In the words of Tupac "keep ya head up" and remember, you are a part of royalty. When I woke you up, I often sang a modified version of this song to you as a child, "rise, shine, give God the glory children, Maxey children of the Lord." I say rise my sons and shine. Move out of your comfort zone and go after your dreams. Don't just talk about it. Be about it. Put the work in to make those dreams become a reality. Yes, it will be hard. Yes, you will be challenged. Yes, you may second guess yourself. Don't be afraid of success. Be yourself and pursue your dreams. God will use our mess, those issues of life, that trauma you experienced and those bad decisions to show your mission in life.

What will you do with the gift of life that God has given you?

Always give of your time, talent, and give back to your community. Remember to reach down and mentor others. Use the power that you hold to fight for injustice.

It has been a privilege to raise all three of you. I was not able to give my aborted child this same opportunity. I made that choice and God has forgiven me, but I wanted to make certain I acknowledge my aborted child.

I love the lyrics from John Legend & The Roots "Shine "I love to see their face. Beautiful minds trapped inside. Let them shine on. Ordinary people can be a hero, don't blow out their light. Let them shine on." Sons, you matter to God, to me, to our family, and to this world (whether they admit it or not). I will end with this poem written by your Auntie Shena.

Dear Black Son,

I would give anything to know that you are protected,

I would give anything to know that you are respected,
But instead, I fear that you will be hunted down

And told that you are less than a man because your skin is brown,

Educate yourself and learn your rights,

Know when to be silent
And know when to use
Your knowledge to fight,

Dear Black Son,

If life continues to give you a shove,

Just know that I am here with open arms,

No Judgment Just Unconditional Love

~Raushena Hill, Auntie

CHAPTER 8

FOR MY THINKING AND SMILING BLACK SONS

BY YOLANDA MUHAMMAD

FOR MY THINKING AND SMILING BLACK SONS
BY YOLANDA MUHAMMAD

I didn't grow up wanting children. I co-raised a set of twin siblings and by the time I was out of college, I had had enough. I was free to do whatever I desired, travel, spend my own money, just enjoy being grown. I joined the Nation of Islam in 1990 and I really felt free. It was a good time to be young and free. I could go on details or assignments; buy garments; and get my hair done every week. I was just enjoying myself.

The first real idea I had about the importance of Mother, I got from a lecture series from Minister Farrakhan, entitled, "How to Give Birth to a God". Funny, a Brother in the Nation, had given me that same lecture series, at an earlier time, as a gift. Hilarious. After studying the lecture series for some time, I began to say this prayer, **"Oh Allah, please bless me to produce children that will be a blessing to you and our family. Children that will be obedient and pleasing to you. Children that will help build our Nation."**

Twenty-five years later I am blessed to help rear a full family of two biological sons, a daughter, nieces, and nephews. I am really somebody's momma. Along with this awesome responsibility, comes the intimate knowledge that this world is not Black-Man-Friendly. So, all my life I have warned my sons about avoiding those Black-Men-Unfriendly zones. Do not wear hoodies! Do not be in the car with more than one other Black Man! If you must be in the car with more than one Black Man, make sure somebody is old or female or both. Never come back to your drink. Never go outside without your ID. Do not trust anyone. Do not talk your business on the phone! Don't post crazy pictures on social media, especially, not ones with guns, money, or strippers. Don't tell anybody where you live at! Please, do not give the family jewels to anybody whose ancestors were not slaves! Constantly, I warned my sons. During one of these intense warning sessions one of my sons screamed out "**Ma, when do I get to be a man**." It hit me so hard, but the result is this love letter.

Dear Son, I never called you boy. You were born a man, wise like an old slave, always plotting the next escape. For 14 days I was in labor. I could not sit down. I could not stand up. I could not sleep, and I could not eat. I went to the hospital six times only to be turned around. On time seven, I was greeted by a doctor from the motherland. He told me I was doing well and that my heart rate would drop and that would be the signal that it was time to deliver. His wisdom and knowledge of pregnancy made me feel so relaxed. I was so big, and I just wanted to secure you from the beginning. We waited and waited. I could not take the pain, so I accepted an epidural in my back. When my heart rate finally dropped my African doctor exited and in came "Dr. 'Becky' with the good hair." Within five minutes, she screamed, "Emergency C-Section", then they wheeled me into the room next door. And then came the stab, followed an 'S-pattern knife-drag in my pelvic area. No mercy, no anesthesia! I am still not convinced that she didn't know, and for a quick minute, I thought she smiled. Nevertheless, the bellowing scream that came from me confirmed that I was feeling every second of the dragging-knife and my terror that she was stabbing my baby.

In my mind, I beat her ass but in reality, I saw you fat, yucky and smiling before I passed out. You weighed 10 pounds 11 ounces with a smile and bright eyes. Your birth set the tone for my level of sacrifice for you. How many women today, can say, "I lived through a real-life, "Roots" experience and survived Dr. Becky's slavery method of delivering babies."

Breast feeding

Sister E was an older Sister in the Mosque, who joined the Nation of Islam in the 1950s under the Honorable Elijah Muhammad. She was one of the 'Mosque Mommas' in Cleveland. When I was pregnant with you, she would pull me to the side every week to teach me some little tidbit about breastfeeding. To be honest, I was in my late twenties, and still wearing training bras. So, from the beginning, I thought you were going to starve to death. I could not figure out if it would be weird to force you to try to nurse. I know it sounds horrible, but it's just something I had to add to my prayer list.

My other 'Mosque Momma', Sister D, joined the bandwagon by telling me that I never had to feed you any food, just breast milk. I was so eager to be a good mother. It's hilarious that I can now say this, but prayer one was answered. I wasn't going to be flat chested for the rest of my life. By the time you were born I had gone from 30B to 38 DD. I breast fed you until you were 15 months old. I hope I didn't scar you for life, but you were so healthy and smart, and your pamper was always full. Prayer two was answered you remained healthy, and I only fed you breast milk. So, I did the right thing.

Son, you were hilarious during that feeding period. When you were about five months old, we were walking downtown in Chicago, and I was having such a hard time carrying you. You were huge. A woman walked up to us to comment on how cute you were. You smiled and reached right into her shirt and grabbed her. I was so embarrassed. When I told your Grandfather he said, "You

90

are making the boy a freak, nobody in this modern time is still breast-feeding children that are as big as him. You should just stop it." I heard this repeatedly, but if Minister Farrakhan said we were all good, you were going to get breast milk, hook, or crook. Today, I'd like to take credit for your amazing immune system and the fact that when everybody else has the flu, you are up and running.

Cursing and Talking all at the same time

I was determined that you would love reading and you would not grow up staring at a television. So, I did certain things with you. We read books, we played with Lego, we made stuff. We talked all the time. We are taught, in the Nation, never to mimic baby-talk with your children, because those are not real words. So, I never did that. I did do a lot of cursing. After the normal first words, 'sh** (expletive)' was your favorite word. It was almost like you knew just when and how to say it. Sometimes you would say it quickly and sometimes you would drag it out. I couldn't stop you. And the more I looked upset, the funnier and more curse-fluent you got. So, I gave up. You said a lot of other good words, and you knew not to embarrass me at the Mosque, so I let it slide. You are the reason all the other children grew up with free curse days.

When you were almost a year old, I let you go to Chicago for a vacation with Grandma. After a day alone with her, she called me. She said, "I think something is wrong with PooMan, he won't stop watching TV. He is like a drug addict; he won't even sleep, and he has pissed on himself twice." I forgot to tell her. So, I said, "Ma he has never watched television. At least not for long periods of time." She paused and then said "What... you... [@! ^! (#! #) (!

91

@#] …him up for the real world. That's why he is sitting here looking crazy."

When you got home, you stared at me as if you wanted to jump me. You looked at me and then the TV and back at me. Then out of your mouth you said, "Grandma said you… [f@#!) @*!) @*] … me up and to let me watch TV." Of course, I spanked you and turned-on National Geographic.

Your Rap Career

Son, you were always brilliant. So, when I asked you, at 5 years old, what you wanted to be and you said a neurologist, I believed you. How dare anyone tell me different? I bought every science toy, book, or outfit I could find. You had stethoscopes, needles, pill bottles. We made hospitals with Lego. We read books about doctors. You had it all.

Imagine how happy I was when your teachers began to tell me you were brilliant in Science and Math. I knew it. When you were a child and you perceived I had a headache, you would lay your hand on my head and say Mommy I can heal you. I knew it. I really was up on "10", when we heard CUBA was giving free scholarships for Medical School. Then you started speaking Spanish. I could see it, Dr. Samad Muhammad at 19, better than Doogie Howser could ever be. So, imagine my surprise when I found out you were sneaking over Sister K's house to become, Doug E Fresh mixed with a little Islamic version of the rapper ODB.

At first, I thought you just loved music. You always have. Your dad and I used to drive you around in the truck with the radio on to get you to go to sleep. When you taught yourself how to play piano, I was so excited. Then you learned to read music, then your pants started sagging. A little weed, fast girls, and late nights followed. Okay, typical teenager stuff. I didn't see it coming. I just thought, Music and Medicine go together, so it's okay.

Now, the first thing I find out, there's no longer any Cuba, for Medical School. You don't want to go. Okay, so, you'll just take the traditional route to medical training. You graduated high school at 15, so you had a little more time. You said you did not like the University of Chicago, because there were no Black men on the school tour. Okay. State school is not that bad. Maybe you will do "gen-ed" classes and then transfer.

Not a bad plan. But one semester in, I found out you were ditching classes to make studio time. It's always someone with a smile who just springs it on you. So, now I'm at the Mosque discovering that you have rap songs on the internet. I didn't know what to do. Do I embrace the rapping? Do I challenge you to a rap battle, what...?

Who did this? Who infiltrated my camp and changed my perfect plan? I think Allah has forgiven me now, but I was mad at a lot of people for at least a year. I hated Kayne for being from Chicago and inspiring people. I hated Jay Z for making it look so easy and cool. I hated Naz and Public Enemy for being so conscious and most of all, I disliked every little fast-behind girl that walked up to us and asked, in that squeaky voice, "Ain't you in NuWorld?"

For a year I listened to smooth jazz only with no words. Then I found out Queen Latifah had a jazz album. Pissed me completely off. Finally, I listened to your first album, and I was mad at myself. I would be driving in the car, blasting it, then I would just turn it off. The nerve of you to rap about going to medical school in Cuba. It was really your Grandmother that helped me get over it and just evolve. She said, "He has a beautiful voice, and he will

93

either grow out of it or become the designated singer at the family reunion. You new mothers. You should really just beat PooMan ass and make him go to college."

Tuskegee

Tuskegee broke me in. When you told me you had a plan, I said I'd support you. Your uncle refined it, by saying "Nephew you only got a couple of years to stay in the family pockets, because there are six others behind you." You were so sure the folks at Tuskegee were telling the truth about the scholarships they said you had. I knew they were lying, but I wanted desperately to have your back. They did promise you a scholarship and housing and all of that. Who knew scholarship meant $500 toward a $23,000 a semester bill? I still remember it like it was yesterday. Your grandfather and I drove all the way down south with you and E's stuff filled to the top of the rental. We had the big breakfast at International House of Pancakes and before we could get out of Alabama, we got the call.

Son: Ma, I need you to come back and sign some stuff
Me: What stuff son?
Son: These papers.
Me: Son, you can read, what do the papers say?
Son: Ma, I'm not sure.
Me: Son, if you can't understand what they say, then they must be loan papers. I told you these people were lying.
Son: Ma – please.

Two things resulted from this. Over the course of two years, I emptied out my savings which wasn't enough. We cried together, cursed together, and prayed some more. I thank Allah that you

94

learned some good life lessons. I prayed you make it out of the Non-Black-Man-friendly environment that colleges can sometimes be. I'm glad that you made it home. The second thing that happened, no one else talked to me about going to a Black college or attending college without a full scholarship.

Marriage and Family – Serious Life

Son, everything that you have done in life has prepared you for right now. Everything you do now is preparing you for tomorrow. You are very blessed in some extraordinary ways, but to whom much is given much is required. You have a heavy burden on your shoulders. But Allah never puts on you more than you can bear.

In the words of my grandfather - a motto that has become our family's creed, "If you don't do no more for your family than I have done, you won't have done nothing."

You are blessed to have been raised in the bosom of some of the greatest thinkers in your cypher? You must always be a thinking man. Your wife and your children to come deserve the best of you.

I know you have a flare for the fabulous, but please balance your life with modesty and humility. Try to listen more. Continue to focus on healthy living and all aspects of the truth. But remember truth, out of season, doesn't have the power as it would, when it is on time. So, keep your mind fluid, disciplined in the now and working towards your future.

You are a great man and there is no one like you ever to exist on the planet or to come. You are a unique individual that is a part of a Nation. A member of the human family who needs to do your part. Be happy. Be honest. Be good to yourself and good to your family. Most importantly, if you fall, get back up. You come from a family of overcomers. From the first day I was blessed to meet you, I knew you were resilient and strong. It doesn't make a difference that "Dr. Becky with the Good Hair" tried to stab us to death. From Day One, and in spite of it, you came out smiling and on top. I love you always and I am immensely proud of you.

My Smiling Black Son

Black is not a color or a race, it is the origin of everything. From the Blackness of space Allah (God) created an entire universe of light, then He **smiled** on it and said it is good. This is you. *Mom remixing scripture and revelation from the Honorable Elijah Muhammad *.*

Love is not a noun. Love is a *verb*. ***The Divine Value of Woman, the Honorable Minister Louis Farrakhan.***

I will always do "something" when it concerns you.

I started my love letters with these two, because they define your very existence. While I may not be able to control or guide your every move, I can do something to exemplify my love. So, I decided to talk to you about your birth and what I desperately admire about you. I want you to always remember that you are unique and there will never be anyone like you. And because you only get one shot at you, make everyday a lesson on being the best you for the next day. Also, remember to be patient with you and love on yourself no matter what circumstance you find yourself in. Nothing happens all at once. Even Allah (God), the creator of the universe, took time to create himself.

On one very rare and honored occasion we were at the home of the Honorable Minister Louis Farrakhan that is now affectionally known as, "The Farm" or "The Garden" and he said, (paraphrasing respectfully) 'the only way we can change our environment, DNA is to follow the teachings of the Most Honorable Elijah Muhammad'. I know this is true. Your whole life I have said to you, I know where you come from. I am not referring to your origin from God, but what we have been shaped into from being in this iniquitous world.

You come from what we all come from. A very gifted, talented, genius family that without discipline and guidance, may do anything that will excite their minds. We are always looking for the challenge or someone to tell us we can't do something – we can't get away with something, we shouldn't do something. Within this same parameter, we are some of the most spiritual, loving, and generous people you could ever meet. We are very principled. Even in BS, we demand integrity. And the best way to get cut from our list, is to steal from us, lie on us, or try to punk us. This, my son, is your ancestry. This, my son, is your parents. This, my son, is you.

You are very loving, very loyal, very sensitive, very generous, very compassionate, very clever, and a defender of the underdog. I love this about you. You also do these things silently and behind the scenes. This is how you were born.

I was nursing your sister for several months, before I even realized I was carrying you. I was uber-sensitive about everything, but I would always hide it. I had two children to make it with, and a funny-life situation. I did not want to worry people, but inside I was begging Allah to just get me to the next phase of whatever. Then I found out I was pregnant. By now, I had already begun to shape your thinking in my wound with this type of passive-let the environment around me plays out-type of attitude. I did my best to change my prayer. And because of this I marked you.

Your first kick in my belly was the early dawn prayer (Fajr). As Allah is my witness, until the day you were born, every morning, you would kick to wake me for morning prayer. If I thought I was not going to get up, you would go off until I got up. You would not calm down until you would hear the melody of the prayer. Your brother dominated my body. Your sister dominated my body. But you and I, we peacefully existed with each other. You only had one requirement, the morning prayer. Even after you were born, I would wake up to find you peeking at me for the prayer.

I was so angry with your father, that I did not want to give you, his name. I wanted to name you after a very pious brother in our nation. But the day you came, you had a full smile and teeth. It was like Allah marked you, with the thing I loved most – the Smile. The night before, I went to the hospital, and it just wasn't time. But it was so hot, and I was so big.

The nurse sympathized with me, and she said, "He seems like a pretty chill baby. Just tell him you are ready for him to come, and he will." So, I did, and you did. At 5 am in the morning we finished prayer and here you come. I had to call the neighbor to watch your brother and sister, and you were pushing right out. We barely made it to the hospital in the ambulance. From the ambulance to the hospital bed and minutes later, my smiling Black son was looking right at me. You were so beautiful. Oh, my Allah, you were so beautiful. You looked so happy to see me and I was happy to see you. That beautiful smile, those new teeth pushing through your gums and all that curly hair. I felt like we were friends.

You wanted everything as if you were grown in age from the beginning. You wanted food instead of breast milk. You wanted to walk instead of crawl. You hated pampers. You always wanted

98

to be with the older children in the family. And even though it seemed you were moving fast; you were very laid back about everything else. I spent so much time, trying to teach you everything. And in your own time, when I thought you were totally frustrated, you would do something to let me know you got it all the time. I recall trying to teach you to write your name. And you would never write it while I was sitting with you. You would just smile, like I was saying nothing. Then one day you just wrote your name like it was nothing. This attitude has marked your whole life. I wish that I would have been paying better attention because I did not see it coming.

I can't tell you what to be or who to be. I already tried this with your siblings, and it did not work. I do know that whatever path you choose, you are going to do whatever you want. You are a mastermind. But I do know that DNA and environment will play a part in your development.

The Nation of Islam was never created to be a mass movement. There are some people that can exist outside the structure of meetings, classes, etc. But there is no one, especially no Black man, that can master this iniquitous world without the Teachings. It just won't happen. I don't care what you call it, the root is God's Law, God's discipline. You were born with several extraordinary gifts, but what will you use them for?

Your smile is so outstanding, I could see the stars when you smiled. With discipline you can use your smile to heal. But in this environment, smiling faces only tell lies. You are very generous. With discipline, your generosity can save many people. In this world, generosity is flipped to become gluttony and theft. You are resilient as hell. But will you use your resilience to improve yourself or just give in to the stereotypes. The stronger your God-potential, the harder it is to fight against the desire to do it your way. This world makes you think your way was created in your own mind. But the truth is Satan has set many traps for a man like you. He fears you in your God-mind but has no fear when we function out of his world.

I can't be a hypocrite and write to you that I have never done anything. Even if I want to tell that lie, there are too many people still living that can prove otherwise. The '100' of the situation is I am you and the only thing that saved me was the Teachings of the Most Honorable Elijah Muhammad. It was and is the only thing that can capture my mind. But son, the good way of life that is the Nation of Islam came to me after everything around me failed and proved untrue. This is the reality that keeps me up at night praying for you. I do not know how far you must go before everything fails you. I don't know how hard you have to fall before you realize you didn't create your own environment. I hope you never have to fall.

I do know it is a trap to keep you in the trap. It's a ceiling and you are not meant to have a ceiling. I wish I could just reach into your dissatisfaction and pull you close to me. I wish that I could just have my praying, smiling, beautiful Black son back in the best of my environment.

I knew the day would come when you would have to make your own way. I remember you asking me, when do I get to be a man. I am with you. But you have to realize this world is not Black-Man-friendly. Not too many people want to see you as the man you were born to be, the beautiful powerful Smiling Servant of the Sovereign Ruler.

You are born to be a father to children, a husband, a protector of women. I have seen this in you on so many occasions. You love people, and people love you. You are so witty and humorous. You are just good people. So, I pray that Allah (God) protects you, while you grow up into the real understanding of yourself. I pray that you get the chance for your mind to grow into harmony with your own universe. I know how powerful you are. You know how powerful you are. They know how powerful you are. As the sunrises, I see your smile and when the sun sets the stars sparkle as a reminder of your brilliance.

Finally, I love you with every drop of my essence. I love every atom of energy that makes you. I am thankful that Allah made me your mother and your first advocate. My love for you is unconditional. I will always feel your presence at every prayer, but I can't wait until I am in the Jummah led by you. This is my Love Letter to My Black Son.

CHAPTER 9

SON OF MINE

BY JONNITA DOCKENS

SON OF MINE
BY JONNITA DOCKENS

Dear Black Son,

Every day, I am overwhelmed that I was chosen to give you life. Your journey from conception to creation is legendary; it almost seems fictional. Historically, men who have the same or a similar story have all become great, well-known men of God. In all occurrences it has been a strong woman who had the responsibility of rearing these men. In my eyes, I was not as strong as any of these women, but I accepted the challenge. Honestly, I always wondered why I was chosen to be your mother.

Motherhood wasn't my specialty. I did not get the set of lessons I think most women learn before becoming a mother. I did not get the chance to help parent younger siblings. I didn't babysit often. The only tools I knew about parenting came from knowing what I didn't want based on my experiences with my parents.

Son, my chosen parenting practice has always been brutal honesty mixed with a little fear. The fear portion was something generational. As the family story goes, your grandparents were nothing to be played with and neither were their parents. So, I always wanted you to know exactly who I was capable of being and who I recovered from being. This was love to me.

My honesty had limits. One of the limits to my honesty was admitting I didn't know if I could be a good parent. I didn't think I had what it took to be a mother, but I wanted children, a husband, and a large family. This unspoken fear stopped me in my tracks on many occasions. Prior to getting pregnant, the doctors told me I would never have children, so you were my miracle birth. As I write you this letter, I realize I was just too damn honest about everything. I talked to you about my gang life. I joined because your uncle told me they wouldn't let me be a member of the gang. I was determined to join and excel. Excelling included doing irrational things like-carrying guns on a regular basis. I was given this task because a nerdy looking young Black girl wouldn't be stopped by the police. During our discussions about my gang life, I always told you how I was blessed to survive. I revealed these stories to you to make you aware that I was not without error. Telling you these stories was also a form of protection. As a Black girl, I could carry a bag of guns and never be stopped and searched, but your uncle, a Black boy, could be searched daily. I could wear gang colors and go unnoticed, but Black boys would be a victim to an illegal inspection and civil rights violation. By sharing these stories, I hoped you understood the hurt and harm I placed on others was unnecessary. Despite my actions toward others, God loved me, still.

Life has a way of giving us situations that cause us to learn an important lesson. In writing this letter to you, I hope to give you clarity on the life lessons I attempted to teach you. This public exchange is a way to share wisdom. My hope is, as you are reading this, the wisdom will open your eyes. Of course, my desire is that my message is so powerful, you are led to share the lessons with other young men your age. Some lessons are so important they last a lifetime. Later in life, son, be sure to share these lessons this with your children. I hope these tools equip you with everything you need to make better choices in the future. As a family we often share memories. It is these memories that have provided some of my greatest lessons.

It's funny how your cousins always bring up the time, I jumped across couches to hem you up. This occasion has been referenced as the matrix. This style of parenting was generational. Your grandparents dished out strict punishment. Their grandparents were stern. When I was a child, I didn't understand that discipline came from a place of love. My love for you included physical chastisement. This was hard for me. I can truly say, being a mother is the hardest job I've ever had. Previously in life, when work was too hard or challenged my beliefs, I would quit. I couldn't write a letter of resignation from motherhood. My goal was to be successful, and parenting was not easy.

For a good portion of your life, my finances were at times like fool's gold, yet it gave you a roof over your head, clothes on your back, and tuition for private school even when I couldn't afford it. I witnessed your grandfather, make his own path, and become his own boss. I chose to establish and build my own empire as well. Now trust, I put in the work, I studied in school, and have a scroll of credentials to prove it. Yes, I have multiple degrees. Son, I've even held positions at top fortune 500 companies that many would have considered hard to get or felt I would not be chosen. However, all of that just wasn't enough! The entrepreneurship journey was for me. Son, listen to your own soul's desires, fulfill the calling that gives you joy. Tearfully, I must admit that being a business owner who was sometimes barely making it was me showing love to you. We each possess our own uniqueness, do not be afraid to step out on faith. I wanted to be the parent who picked you up from school and showed up for your chess tournaments. However, I didn't want to be a punk parent and I always questioned if you understood my love. Amid trying to be this strong Black single mother, I wanted you to know that I love you. During periods of your life, you would tell me that I was strange, because I would randomly just say I love you. Son of mine, I was committed to telling you I love you often. I wanted you to understand that there is 'no charge' for my love. I give it to you freely and without conditions. Telling you I love you was my mission, and this showed up in many ways including the corny notes I wrote to you. Those were my expressions of unconditional love to you.

Son, you have always been independent. As a child, you were always surrounded by other children, but you've always been your own person. Other children didn't influence your path, you were grounded and did your own thing. There was always a minimum of seven or more children with me. We mastered how to ride deep in a car. You were the life of the party at an early age. But you always made time to enjoy your own company. Hold tight and never lose sight of putting yourself first. One night, your grandfather came to visit, and he stayed overnight. I was asleep and in the late hours of the night after everyone was asleep you got up. You were riding your big wheel in the dark. I didn't hear you riding but I woke up to your grandfather cursing. He was cursing you out and screaming go the fuck to bed. Honestly, he sounded like the Mississippi Burning version of Samuel Jackson. Then he started screaming at me. Of course, I was flustered and trying to figure out what was going on. Well, you were riding your big wheel in the dark and he thought you were a burglar who had entered our home. It was dark and he couldn't see your face. Somehow, in the dark, he grabbed a bat and was in full swing when he turned the light on. You said "granddabby where is the ball"? I can look back now and say, you live by the beat of your own drum! Even if you are the only one to hear the music. It is a trait many have lost along their way. You really loved to play by yourself, watch television by yourself, and read books by yourself.

Even though you were independent you would always welcome a companion to join in on your fun. From childhood to pre-teen to becoming a teenager, your idea of fun changed, and I wasn't ready for my baby who was growing into a man. In a parent's eye you never want your children to leave the nest, but it's necessary.

The first time I wrote you a love letter it was super cold outside. I did this because it seemed to me that saying I love you every other day wasn't enough. You were starting to grow into the next phase of yourself and I really didn't know how to deal with who you were becoming. You see, "I had to get this right". On your 10th birthday, my thoughts were, does my Black son understand that I love him deeply. In the midst of trying to be a good parent, I was also trying to be a provider, be active in the community, and have a social life. I was always spearheading, numerous afterschool programs. So, while on the go, I crafted these notes that started with little quick tears of paper and jotting down a few words of encouragement. There was a short love letter when you had a test coming up. A letter came after I disciplined you. A love letter arrived when your mood was a little off. A letter appeared when you wouldn't share how you were feeling. I was always curious to know if you understood that I love you. God blessed me by allowing me to be your mother. Throughout your life I wanted to make sure you heard me say the words I love you. As your mother, I was committed to saying these words to you and will for the rest of our lives.

Watching you grow older was a joy. This joy was filled with love, laughter, and tears. You always had this happy- go-lucky comical presence. I don't know when it happened, but this little funny child was turning 10. During this phase of your life, I started writing more notes and love letters. TEN! This is when the tears began to flood. Oscar Grant was a Black son who was killed shortly after your birthday. His death at the hands of a police officer was major news. This news caused me to have a variety of emotions. Reality and fear ran rampant in my mind during- this phase of your life. You were not just Jaylen; you were my Black son. This is the point where I really understood that the world would see you as a threat not as my Black son. I would encourage you in one sentence and tell you to be careful in the next. This is the stage of our lives where I got the first glimpse of you becoming a man. Daily, I reinforced through my words and actions that I loved you. My conversations with you became more about living as a Black man. My heart ached because I wanted you to know about love, not hate.

For Black sons, the world tries to define who you are or who you are expected to become. This love that I have for you always puts me in protector mode. I wanted to shelter you from the harm you couldn't understand. Of course, all my life's training said make sure your child is well educated because that is love. So, we sent you to catholic school. St. Columbanus was an extremely popular catholic school in Chicago with a tremendous success rate. Your father and I decided this was the place to educate you. So, from kindergarten through third grade I missed hearing you were "BAD AS HELL"! It wasn't because I was not present. I wasn't on the PTA, but I volunteered for functions. I picked up your report card. I scheduled meetings with your teachers. I was on the committee for the Taste of St. C (the local school fundraiser that was a neighborhood version of the Taste of Chicago). Your mother was continually active, and you were still acting out. Ultimately, I missed hearing-you were a handful even though I was there. Now, I laugh because you spent most of second grade in Dr. Wadlington's third grade class. Like most people who encounter you, she loved and still loves you. She never said you were bad, and I never comprehended that you were a lot to handle. My thought was they need a better second grade teacher. St. Columbanus had one Black man who worked at the school. All the women at the school thought you were so adorable. All-female teachers along with your behavior issues seemed to be why you weren't achieving the quality educational results desired. Son, I love that you were too much for the second-grade teacher because almost two decades later my understanding of you is painting a clearer picture. Your personality was developing, and I was present physically but not in the moment mentally. In hindsight, I grew to understand that growth and development looks different for everybody, and you were not exempt. One day you will have your own family, recall moments in time like these as teachable ones.

This is when I decided to send you to Muhammad University of Islam (MUI). Your father did not like that decision. Your stubborn mother didn't care what he didn't like. When he told me he wouldn't pay for tuition at MUI, I told your dad I was not a whore for education dollars and enrolled you in school. Yes, I am the Black mother who acts up over her Black son's education. I knew the mold was broken when I had you, you were a leader, and not a paper cutout. Deep in my heart, I knew God had a purpose for your life beyond my understanding. Silently, I prayed and asked God for direction. All the time, I was wondering if MUI, is the place where God will connect you to your purpose. As a mother I left no stone unturned! When it came to you, there is no telling what I would or wouldn't do, and my feelings are still as strong today as they were then.

My love for you said put your son around some men he can't punk out. For me, MUI represented good education, good men, and BLACKNESS. I was extremely excited about you and MUI.

I knew you wouldn't be able to flash that winning smile and use your amazing charm with these teachers. They were legendary for educating the best of the best and being no nonsense. During what I will call your MUI years, I saw you growing up.

While your dad and I didn't agree on MUI, I made a decision and a commitment that school officials were not allowed to discipline you in any form. I had meetings because you didn't have detention and your strong personality didn't go unnoticed. In most of these meetings the Dean would compliment you and list your accolades. The Dean loved all the things I loved about you. He would tell me, "Jaylen is a natural leader"! He wasn't the only one who sang your praises and shared my love for you. Your science teacher said you gave her the blues, but she also told me you were very independent and had the ability to influence your peers. I love that you possess those qualities. The principal reported that you were very respectful and had a great sense of humor. In all these meetings, the thing that was consistent was that I was not the only one who loved you. It's true what you put out comes back to you, I could have not asked for a more precious gift than you.

Son, I love you for many reasons because you made me a better person. School, work, and making friends were all easy to me. Being a parent was something that challenged every aspect of my life. Before you, there were areas of my life that I felt allowed me to make free and sometimes reckless decisions. My love for you enabled me to make better choices and sound choices. Throughout your life, I have confessed these honest decisions. Prayerfully, I hope that you heard me, and understood my love.

I am your mother. While my demonstrations of love may be strange, I am okay with that. As you continue to grow into being your own Black man, I need to reiterate lessons previously taught and lessons I hope you learn:

1. **Black sons are seen as a threat - don't let what the world thinks about you define you.** Society wants you to believe Black men are a threat. The media portrays young men as a nemesis and suggests even old people should be fearful in your presence. Don't buy into that frame of thinking. Too many Police Officers and old white people jump to immediate stereotypical thoughts that a young Black man must be involved in violence or drugs. Son, you know who you are. Everywhere you go, stand armed with your truth.

2. **YOU ARE ENOUGH!** Music has been a false influence. It has impacted and helped determine that you must be among the who's who to be somebody. You must be dressed fly. You are defined by the material things that one acquires in life. As you know all those things are materialistic, their value could never measure up to the amount of a person's life worth. You must define who you are. Define yourself by your character and daily actions.

3. **"Be a thinking man!"** These are your grandmother's infamous words to the men in our family. Before you take action, think first, and then move. It is important to tap into your immediate surroundings, make an assessment, and then execute. Think before moving and then take your own pathway.

4. **Pray without ceasing!** Son may your thirst for life forever be quenched with prayer. Always pray in everything that you do! In every way take time and then allow yourself to

ask for guidance. Be willing to speak your dreams and desires to the Most High. You will be blessed and provided with guidance and the steps to take to bring your dreams and desires to life.

5. **Don't ever put your hands on a woman!** This is a non-negotiable! Let your yes be yes, and your no be no! When in a relationship there may be a time you want to strike, don't. It is NEVER going to work in your favor. Be willing to walk away from a relationship that isn't working, and no it is not a 'punk ass' move either! The odds are most often not in your favor as a Black man. Just know you can always start again.

6. **Challenges come in all shapes and sizes.** They are always right in your face. If you can avoid harming someone else, avoid it at all costs. There use to be a street code that man lived by and it would be handled by the two and then life went on. Today, it's best to take the road less traveled and don't look back. You must be a bigger person. You have the power to choose and not let your talents go to waste.

7. **Men are the maintainers of women and children**. Take care of your family. You have a responsibility to make provision emotionally, spiritually, financially, physically. It is never enough to just make a child and not pour into their future. What you put in; you get in return. Children replicate what they see! Too many times in history adults say you do as I say, not as I do. That shit ain't gonna work! Be the same in everything you do! I always want you to be solid in all your ways, let your yes be yes and your no be NO or HELL NO! Children witness the way you relate to your mate. Teach your children to live in harmony. This will help them to navigate through life and with people.

Relationships are layered, like an onion. Each layer has its purpose. Family life has it trials. All trials are not bad. Everything isn't always negative or detrimental. Take the lesson and move on. Do not spend time living and regretting what you did not do or to compare your outcomes to any other family. Teach yours to be a strong family unit. To be a resource to each other.

8. **Think before you speak!** It is imperative that you take the time to pause before you speak! The scripture says, As a Man Thinketh, so is he in his heart! Who you are at your core, will be revealed when you speak. Take a moment to reflect upon whatever has been asked of you. It's NOT just what comes to mind. There will be times that your words may evoke judgement or even comments from those around you!! There may even be moments when you REALLY want to say, "MOVE BITCH" GET OUT MY WAY!!! Be mindful whether you are totally in agreement or just pissed off. You get to take control of YOU, that's it! The narrative is yours to write.

9. **When you are angry, Count to ten!** Understanding your own temperament is valuable and a lesson that will last a lifetime. Once upon a time the 'go to' was to beat someone's ASS! There is no room for this today. Many are too lazy to stand up in the world as real man to man, isolated situations so, you must be the BIGGER person. I used to fight way too MUCH! Counting to ten has helped me change my temperament and my spirit. It can help you too.

10. **No Cheap Labor! You are nobody's slave...do not allow yourself to be enslaved in any form**. Today's prison is the breeding ground for free labor. Creating your own

pathway is the key to eternal freedom. Make sure you are paid what you are worth. Invest in your interest, your time is valuable. The one thing that we all have is Time! The difference is what you choose to do with your time. What is it that makes your heart sing? Remember to DREAM! DREAM big, explore and never be fearful to try it again and again. Son, fall forward and know there is always 'blessings' in the lessons. You are worthy!

11. **Be honest with yourself and those around you.** The worst thing anyone can do, is to point the finger and blame someone else. Own up to your situation! Own your mistakes. Tell your truths. If you are wrong, correct yourself, then move on "let that shit go!" Honesty never backfires, it sets everyone free.

12. **Enjoy life.** It's important to be serious sometimes. Don't allow the seriousness of life to make you forget to enjoy each day. Visit new places. Try new things. Ride a bike. Go to a theme party. Take your family on a vacation. Eat a different type of food. Take your date to a comedy show. Spend the entire day watching movies. Just have fun because you can.

Son of mine, I have always valued our relationship. I was chosen to be your mother and you were chosen to be my son. I LOVE YOU! May these words forever guide you through this journey called life!

ACKNOWLEDGEMENTS

This anthology started with an idea and a phone call. One phone call led to two phone calls and on and on. Phone calls lead to emails and emails led to a compilation of expression of love to Black Sons. While each author worked hard this project isn't just about the authors.

We would like to acknowledge our family, friends and industry professionals that helped us bring this vision from a phone call to a published work. Of course, we start with thanking our sons for being the motivation behind these sentiments of love. Some of these chapters include personal stories that are not only about our lives as authors but also include unshared experiences from the lives of our sons. Beyond our sons, we each have family members and friends helped us in numerous ways and we are thankful for their support.

This project was not a solo mission and could not have happened with the support of an amazing professional team.

Dr. Malika Carter, thank you for being our writing coach. Your support of this project and guidance gave us the tools needed to pour our hearts out on paper. Dr. Carter inspires positive systemic change and incorporate social justice methodology into the very fabric of K-12, non-profit, business, and post-secondary institutions. You can contact her and learn more about her work by visiting www.Passion4Pivot.com

Dara Alston, thank you for adding your professional skills to our project. Everybody needs an editor. We appreciate your service as an editor. Sharing your skills with us made our work better. You can learn more about her work at www.avenue89.co.

Sultan Muhammad, thank you for being an intricate part of our editorial team. Your editing services and suggestions were a priceless addition to this work. Through the ashes you could see the potential for this book. Your willingness to uphold your word and guide us through this process gave us the strength and confidence to see it through to its completion. Your entrepreneurial spirit and unwavering empowerment of women

Terry Richard-Williams, thank you for being a part of our team. Your editing services helped each of us improve our love letter. In addition, to editing you made suggestions that helped to improve the overall project. We are thankful for your guidance. You can contact her by email terry@yeswithpes.com or visiting her website www.yeswithpes.com.

Hannibal Muhammad, thank you for being an integral part of this team. What is a book without out a cover? Your patience and guidance were needed. You participated in this book project as if it was your own. You never stopped sharing and extending help. We appreciate your contribution.

In addition to our writing coach, and editors, we had a dynamic photography team to help us capture precious moments for this project. We would like to thank the following photographers for their contribution to this project:

- Michael Kirkland can be reached at www.mjkirkland.com.
- David Myto can be reached at www.mytostudios.com.
- Naiya Rutledge can be reached at naiyshoots@gmail.com

www.ingramcontent.com/pod-product-compliance
Lightning Source LLC
Chambersburg PA
CBHW051145020726
47501CB00005B/1686